New Exploring God's Word

Study Guide

By John Scharlemann

CPH.

Concordia Publishing House

Edited by Thomas J. Doyle

Write to the Library for the Blind, 1333 S. Kirkwood Road, St. Louis, MO 63122-7295 to obtain this study in braille or large print for the visually impaired.

3   4   5   6   7   8   9   10   06   05   04   03   02   01

Contents

Introduction

The study of the New Testament is nothing less than an exploration into the thoughts and desires of God for ordinary people like you and me. It takes us from this hardened and selfish world into the promise of a world where God's peace, justice, and mercy will be complete.

Delving into the Bible for the first time can be somewhat intimidating. We are taken to a distant past which is full of unfamiliar customs and traditions. We must become acquainted with a nation which viewed the world differently than many people do today. And we must begin to alter some of our current definitions to grasp the full meaning of our Lord's love and compassion.

As foreign as many customs and traditions might seem to us today, we will discover that people's natures remain the same. We are trapped today—as people were centuries ago—in an imperfect world where evil and pain seem all too prevalent. We, too, can view the world as meaningless and without hope. But Jesus Christ came to rescue the world from its quagmire, and His deliverance continues to change our lives. Pray that the Word of God, will begin to alter your perspective. May His promises give you rich and lasting hope despite the evil which seems to surround us. And may you find in the midst of current suffering—joy!

How to Use This Study

The Study Guide will direct your study of the New Testament. The typical lesson is divided into six parts:

1. Approaching This Study
2. An Overview
3. The Message in Brief
4. Working with the Text
5. Applying the Message
6. Taking the Message Home

"Approaching This Study" is intended to whet the reader's appetite for the topics at hand. It leads participants into the world of the New Testament while summarizing the issues to be examined. The

"Overview" summarizes the textual material used in each lesson. Before the text is examined in detail, it is viewed as a whole, allowing participants to "see the forest" before "exploring the trees." "The Message in Brief" summarizes the focus of study for the lesson. "Working with the Text" draws participants into deeper biblical study, encouraging them to discover the gems of universal truth which lie in the details of God's Word. When questions appear difficult or unclear, the Leaders Guide provides a doorway to the answers. "Applying the Message" leads participants from the recorded Word of God to its possible application in our present lives. It helps participants more fully realize the implications of God's Word to the daily experience of a Christian. Finally, "Taking the Message Home" invites participants to continue their scriptural meditation at home. Suggestions are given for personal reflection, for preview of the following lesson, and for private study of topics raised by the lesson. The study of God's Word will be greatly enhanced by those actively pursuing the suggestions offered in this section.

Each lesson includes some "trivia" which is intended to spark interest and generate additional discussion. This can be used to develop inquisitiveness and enthusiasm about related issues ripe for exploration.

A glossary is provided at the end of this Bible study. Because a study of the New Testament will lead participants to language that may occasionally seem foreign and difficult, the glossary will make participants more comfortable with terms, phrases, and customs in the Christian church. It will help them understand biblical concepts such as *love* and *grace* which may differ from current definitions.

The Bible study also incorporates easy-to-read charts and maps which will aid participants in their understanding of biblical geography and chronology. These should be referred to frequently during the Bible study as they give visual support to the context of the lesson.

Session 1

God Is Talking to You!

Approaching This Study

Can you imagine the thought of God speaking to YOU? What would He say? What would He want to tell you?

God has given us a book that shares His thoughts and activities in our world to reveal His mercy and compassion. It is called the Bible. He used a number of individuals to record His words in the Bible. These authors who wrote by inspiration of the Holy Spirit came from diverse backgrounds, were born in various parts of the Near East, and lived in different ages, but they all gave us one clear message: God will save His people.

God speaks to us through His Word recorded in Scripture for the purpose of telling about our dilemma of sin and His gift of salvation through Jesus Christ. God wants us to know that the problems of our world are the result of sin, and that we can be freed from the eternal consequences of sin only by God's love and grace through faith in Jesus who willingly went to the cross for our sins.

The Bible has been around for more than 2,000 years. Yet the Holy Spirit continues to bring new life to people through its message. Many who read its pages find a genuine and lasting source of peace and joy. Of course, in order for the Bible to make a difference in our lives, we will have to read it. When we read about His love and compassion, we will begin to understand that we are special creatures. We are not people who serve a meaningless role in an empty world; we are God's children for whom He has a unique purpose and place.

Consider the following Bible verses. What are we asked to do in each verse? What do they have to say about the value of God's Word? What promises does God give to those who follow His commands?

1. "Give ear and come to Me; hear Me, that your soul may live. I will make an everlasting covenant with you, My faithful love promised to David." Isaiah 55:3

2. "To the Jews who had believed Him, Jesus said, 'If you hold to My teaching, you are really My disciples. Then you will know the truth, and the truth will set you free.' " John 8:31–32

obedience

holding to truth

3. "Let the word of Christ dwell in you richly as you teach and admonish one another with all wisdom, and as you sing psalms, hymns and spiritual songs with gratitude in your hearts to God." Colossians 3:16

worship

4. "Your word is a lamp to my feet and a light for my path." Psalm 119:105

5. "I am not ashamed of the gospel, because it is the power of God for the salvation of everyone who believes: first for the Jew, then for the Gentile." Romans 1:16

Jesus is only way to salvation

Gospel = good news

God was not content simply to write about His grace and mercy. Somehow He needed to demonstrate the depth of His love. He wanted us to understand and experience more fully His compassion. And so He sent His Son, Jesus, to die for the sins of the world.

Parents can rarely express the depth of their feelings for their sons

8

and daughters. Children can frustrate, exasperate, and irritate, but they remain the most important object of their parents' love. God knows that. He knows how much we love our children because He is our Creator. In the ultimate demonstration of His love, God sent His one and only Son, Jesus, to suffer the indignities and humiliations of a fallen world and to die on a cross for the sins of fallen humanity. There could be no greater demonstration of the extent of God's love for us than this.

In the New Testament portion of the Bible we read about the life and ministry of God's Son, Jesus. Included in the account is His miraculous birth, His marvelous healing ministry, His sacrificial death, and His earth-shattering resurrection. Whereas the Old Testament writers constantly looked forward to the coming of Jesus Christ, the New Testament describes His arrival and work on the earth. It also reveals how Jesus created and sustained His Church through the power of His Spirit.

An Overview

Read 2 Timothy 3:16–17; 2 Peter 1:20–21, John 20:31. How would you describe the difference between the great works of human literature and the words of Scripture? What is the source of Scripture and what is its purpose? *inspired word of God*

All Scripture is God-breathed and is useful for teaching, rebuking, correcting and training in righteousness. 2 Timothy 3:16

Above all, you must understand that no prophecy of Scripture came about by the prophet's own interpretation. For prophecy never had its origin in the will of man, but men spoke from God as they were carried *(moved)* along by the Holy Spirit. 2 Peter 1:20–21

But these are written that you may believe that Jesus is the Christ, the Son of God, and that by believing you may have life in His name. John 20:31 *Holy Spirit*

The Message in Brief

It is important to understand the Bible's source of authority. It is not "inspired" merely in the sense of possessing beautiful language and poetry such as can be found in the works of Shakespeare or John Milton. It is "inspired" in the sense of being "God-breathed." Within its words are contained the very source of salvation for the human soul. Just as God breathed life into a lump of clay and brought Adam to life, so the words of Scripture bring spiritual life to dead souls. Spiritual life is given through faith in the death and resurrection of Jesus Christ.

Working with the Text

1. In your own words, give a description of how Adam was created by God in Genesis 2:7? What material did God use? What was Adam's source of life? *clay, breath = spirit*

> The LORD God formed the man from the dust of the ground and breathed into his nostrils the breath of life, and the man became a living being. Genesis 2:7

2. What happened when Jesus breathed on the disciples in John 20:22? What did they receive and what were they empowered to do?

> And with that He breathed on them and said, "Receive the Holy Spirit." John 20:22

power to forgive and retain sins

3. How were the disciples empowered by the "wind" of God's Spirit in Acts 2:1–12?

> When the day of Pentecost came, they were all together in one place. Suddenly a sound like the blowing of a violent wind came from heaven and filled the whole house where they were sitting. They saw what seemed to be tongues of fire that separated and came to rest on each of

them. All of them were filled with the Holy Spirit and began to speak in other tongues as the Spirit enabled them.

Now there were staying in Jerusalem God-fearing Jews from every nation under heaven. When they heard this sound, a crowd came together in bewilderment, because each one heard them speaking in his own language. Utterly amazed, they asked: "Are not all these men who are speaking Galileans? Then how is it that each of us hears them in his own native language? Parthians, Medes and Elamites; residents of Mesopotamia, Judea and Cappadocia, Pontus and Asia, Phrygia and Pamphylia, Egypt and the parts of Libya near Cyrene; visitors from Rome (both Jews and converts to Judaism); Cretans and Arabs—we hear them declaring the wonders of God in our own tongues!" Amazed and perplexed, they asked one another, "What does this mean?" Acts 2:1–12

ruah = spirit, wind, breath
↳ Hebrew
Greek word is pneuma = wind, spirit

4. Interestingly, the Hebrew and Greek words for "spirit," "breath," and "wind" are all the same. Knowing this, what other words could you use to describe the life-creating power given Adam? The power given to the disciples when Jesus "breathed" on them? The power given the disciples at Pentecost?

Spirit of God

5. The Greek word which we translate "inspired" literally means "God-breathed." What does this suggest about the power of God's "inspired" words of Scripture? What does the Bible bring to the human soul?

6. Read the following Bible verses and describe how God spoke through His writers:

[a] When Moses went and told the people all the LORD's words and laws, they responded with one voice, "Everything the LORD has said we will do." Moses then wrote down everything the LORD had said. He got up early the next morning and built an altar at the foot of the mountain and set up twelve stone pillars representing the twelve tribes of Israel. Exodus 24:3–4

[b] This is the word that came to Jeremiah from the LORD: "This is what the LORD, the God of Israel, says: 'Write in a book all the words I have spoken to you. The days are coming,' declares the LORD, 'when I will bring My people Israel and Judah back from captivity and restore them to the land I gave their forefathers to possess,' says the LORD." Jeremiah 30:1–3

[c] And He said to me, "Son of man, eat what is before you, eat this scroll; then go and speak to the house of Israel." So I opened my mouth, and He gave me the scroll to eat.

Then He said to me, "Son of man, eat this scroll I am giving you and fill your stomach with it." So I ate it, and it tasted as sweet as honey in my mouth.

He then said to me: "Son of man, go now to the house of Israel and speak My words to them." Ezekiel 3:1–4

[d] And we also thank God continually because, when you received the word of God, which you heard from us, you accepted it not as the word of men, but as it actually is, the word of God, which is at work in you who believe. 1 Thessalonians 2:13

[e] Then I heard a voice from heaven say, "Write: Blessed are the dead who die in the Lord from now on." "Yes," says the Spirit, "they will rest from their labor, for their deeds will follow them." Revelation 14:13

7. Read Exodus 31:18, Exodus 34:1, and Daniel 5:5. Has God ever written anything without the use of human hands? How does the Bible describe the appearance of His writings?

When the LORD finished speaking to Moses on Mount Sinai, He gave him the two tablets of the Testimony, the tablets of stone inscribed by the finger of God. Exodus 31:18

The LORD said to Moses, "Chisel out two stone tablets like the first ones, and I will write on them the words that were on the first tablets, which you broke." Exodus 34:1

Suddenly the fingers of a human hand appeared and wrote on the plaster of the wall, near the lampstand in the royal palace. The king watched the hand as it wrote. Daniel 5:5

Applying the Message

1. The Bible continues to be the best-selling book in the world. It has been translated into hundreds of languages and has been a source of comfort for untold millions. How do you think most people view the Bible? Is it considered something which will merely give a "lift" to the human spirit? Why do you think God intended it to be far more than a guide for good morals?

2. Read Psalm 119:105–112. How can the Word of God be a light for your path? Is God's Word something which will change in time or will it be a constant in your life?

> Your word is a lamp to my feet
>> and a light for my path.
> I have taken an oath and confirmed it,
>> that I will follow Your righteous laws.
> I have suffered much;
>> preserve my life, O LORD, according to Your word.
> Accept, O LORD, the willing praise of my mouth,
>> and teach me Your laws.
> Though I constantly take my life in my hands,
>> I will not forget Your law.
> The wicked have set a snare for me,
>> but I have not strayed from Your precepts.
> Your statutes are my heritage forever;
>> they are the joy of my heart.
> My heart is set on keeping Your decrees
>> to the very end. Psalm 119:105–112

3. When would be a good time for you to study your Bible? What kinds of distractions will you have and how can you limit those distractions?

4. Whom do you know that studies the Bible regularly? Do you think it makes a difference in his or her life? Explain how.

5. President Woodrow Wilson once said: "When you have read the Bible, you will know it is the Word of God, because you will have found

it the key to your heart, your own happiness, and your own duty." In your own words, what does this suggest will happen to you if you regularly study God's Word?

6. Read John 3:16 and explain the purpose of God's work among us. How does this demonstrate the depth of His love? God sacrificed His only child on our behalf. What does this say about your value in God's eyes that He allowed His only Son to die for your sins?

"For God so loved the world that He gave His one and only Son, that whoever believes in Him shall not perish but have eternal life." John 3:16

Taking the Message Home

Review

Read again 2 Timothy 3:16–17, 2 Peter 1:20–21, and John 20:31 in the Overview section. Consider again the important difference between the words of Scripture and other human writings. Consider when you will set aside time for regular and consistent Bible study. Pray for the Lord's strength to maintain your commitment to grow in the Word. Ask the Lord to work through His Word so that you will grow in faith and love towards Him.

Looking Ahead

Read Revelation 22:18–19 and think about the precious nature of God's Word. Consider how we are able to protect His Word—so that it is not lost or changed.

Working Ahead

The following are suggestions for additional study at home.

1. Make a list of those qualities which you admire most in your son or daughter. If you are not a parent, make a list of those positive quali-

ties you find in your mother or father. Spend some time considering what characteristics you would miss most if you were to lose a loved one. Having contemplated such a horrible loss, begin to reflect on what it would mean for God the Father to lose His one and only Son.

2. Ask the pastor and members of your congregation what the Word of God means to them. Ask them which biblical passages are their favorite and which have been most meaningful in their lives. Find out which book of the Bible they think would be the best to study in depth.

Did you know that the oldest, most complete, best known manuscript of the Bible is called the "Codex Sinaiticus"? It was written in the first half of the fourth century after Christ. It was found in 1859 by a German scholar named Tischendorf at the monastery of St. Catherine on Mount Sinai. Parts of it had been placed in a basket of leaves set aside to be burned!

The Codex Sinaiticus (below) is written in Greek. It contains more than 340 pages and measures 15″ x 13½″. The codex form is the forerunner of our modern-day books. It was much easier to use than the long scrolls common in Jesus' day.

Manuscript 43725, folios 235v–236, by permission of the British Library.

The Resurrection by Gustave Doré

And the angel answered and said unto the women, "Fear not ye: for I know that ye seek Jesus, which was crucified. He is not here: for He is risen, as He said. Come, see the place where the Lord lay." (Matthew 28:5–6 KJV). From *The Doré Bible Illustrations*. By permission of Dover Publications, Inc.

Session 2

Getting to the Heart of God's Word

Matthew 28:1–7; Mark 16:1–8; Luke 24:1–12; John 20:1–18

Approaching This Study

The coming of Jesus Christ, His ministry, death, and resurrection are at the center of the Bible. All Scripture points to Jesus. He is so important because through His death and resurrection God provides us that which He promised to the first sinners, Adam and Eve—a Savior. Jesus our Savior lived a perfect life according to God's Law. Jesus, then, received the punishment for our sin when He suffered and died on the cross. Jesus rose from the dead proclaiming victory for us over sin and death. If the Bible omitted Jesus, there would be little point to the book. It should be no surprise that we are given four accounts of Jesus' ministry written by four men who loved Him and followed Him. Inspired by the Holy Spirit Matthew, Mark, Luke, and John recorded their true and accurate knowledge of Jesus' life in the four "Gospels." The four different perspectives provide us a more complete picture of who Jesus was and why He came. One gospel writer, for example, demonstrated how Jesus fulfilled Old Testament prophecy. Another focused on His grace, how He lived and died for all people, Jew and Gentile, man and woman, young and old. Still another emphasized how He was the Son of God. And yet another underscored Jesus' ministry as a source of wonder and amazement.

As we read each account, the writer's perspective becomes more apparent. Look up the following Bible passages and state at least one of each of the author's emphases.

   1. Matthew 2:1–6; 21:1–5; 22:41–45; 26:31–35

2. Mark 1:21–28; 7:31–37; 10:17–27

3. Luke 1:1–4; 10:24; 19:10; 24:45–47,

4. John 1:1,3,14; 20:31

The four gospels are easy to read. They simply tell us what happened during Jesus' life. In the gospels, Jesus tells us many things about sin and forgiveness. He heals many people from spiritual and physical illness, and He discusses His relationship with the Father and the Holy Spirit. It's only when we understand the life and ministry of Jesus that the rest of the Bible begins to make sense.

Look at the following accounts and describe how they picture the same event from different perspectives:

1. Matthew 4:12–17 and Mark 1:14–15

2. Mark 9:2–10 and Luke 9:28–36

3. Matthew 14: 22–31 and John 6:16–21

Resurrection Appearances

EVENT	DATE	Matthew	Mark	Luke	John	Acts	I Corinthians
At the empty tomb outside Jerusalem	Early Sunday morning	28:1-10	16:1-8	24:1-12	20:1-9		
To Mary Magdalene at the tomb	Early Sunday morning		16:9-11		20:11-18		
To two travelers on the road to Emmaus	Sunday at midday		16:12-13	24:13-32			
To Peter in Jerusalem	During the day on Sunday			24:34			15:5
To the ten disciples in the upper room	Sunday evening			24:36-43	20:19-25		
To the eleven disciples in the upper room	One week later		16:14		20:26-31		15:5
To seven disciples fishing on the Sea of Galilee	One day at daybreak				21:1-23		
To the eleven disciples on the mountain in Galilee	Some time later	28:16-20	16:15-18				
To more than 500	Some time later						15:6
To James	Some time later						15:7
At the Ascension on the Mt. of Olives	Forty days after the resurrection			24:44-49		1:3-8	

Taken from NIV STUDY BIBLE. Copyright © 1985 by the Zondervan Corporation. Used by permission of Zondervan Publishing House.

An Overview

Read the four accounts of Jesus' resurrection in Matthew 28:1-7; Mark 16:1-8; Luke 24:1-12; and John 20:1-18. Notice how some of the details in each account seem to differ.

> After the Sabbath, at dawn on the first day of the week, Mary Magdalene and the other Mary went to look at the tomb.
>
> There was a violent earthquake, for an angel of the Lord came down from heaven and, going to the tomb, rolled back the stone and sat on it. His appearance was like lightning, and his clothes were white as snow. The guards were so afraid of him that they shook and became like dead men.
>
> The angel said to the women, "Do not be afraid, for I know that you are looking for Jesus, who was crucified. He is not here; He has risen, just as He said. Come and see the place where He lay. Then go quickly and tell His disciples: 'He has risen from the dead and is going ahead of you into Galilee. There you will see Him.' Now I have told you." Matthew 28:1-7

> When the Sabbath was over, Mary Magdalene, Mary the mother of James, and Salome bought spices so that they might go to anoint Jesus' body. Very early on the first day of the week, just after sunrise, they were

on their way to the tomb and they asked each other, "Who will roll the stone away from the entrance of the tomb?"

But when they looked up, they saw that the stone, which was very large, had been rolled away. As they entered the tomb, they saw a young man dressed in a white robe sitting on the right side, and they were alarmed.

"Don't be alarmed," he said. "You are looking for Jesus the Nazarene, who was crucified. He has risen! He is not here. See the place where they laid Him. But go, tell His disciples and Peter, 'He is going ahead of you into Galilee. There you will see Him, just as He told you.' "

Trembling and bewildered, the women went out and fled from the tomb. They said nothing to anyone, because they were afraid. Mark 16:1–8

On the first day of the week, very early in the morning, the women took the spices they had prepared and went to the tomb. They found the stone rolled away from the tomb, but when they entered, they did not find the body of the Lord Jesus. While they were wondering about this, suddenly two men in clothes that gleamed like lightning stood beside them. In their fright the women bowed down with their faces to the ground, but the men said to them, "Why do you look for the living among the dead? He is not here; He has risen! Remember how He told you, while He was still with you in Galilee: 'The Son of Man must be delivered into the hands of sinful men, be crucified and on the third day be raised again.' " Then they remembered His words.

When they came back from the tomb, they told all these things to the Eleven and to all the others. It was Mary Magdalene, Joanna, Mary the mother of James, and the others with them who told this to the apostles. But they did not believe the women, because their words seemed to them like nonsense. Peter, however, got up and ran to the tomb. Bending over, he saw the strips of linen lying by themselves, and he went away, wondering to himself what had happened. Luke 24:1–12

Early on the first day of the week, while it was still dark, Mary Magdalene went to the tomb and saw that the stone had been removed from the entrance. So she came running to Simon Peter and the other disciple, the one Jesus loved, and said, "They have taken the Lord out of the tomb, and we don't know where they have put Him!"

So Peter and the other disciple started for the tomb. Both were running, but the other disciple outran Peter and reached the tomb first. He bent over and looked in at the strips of linen lying there but did not go in. Then Simon Peter, who was behind him, arrived and went into the tomb. He saw the strips of linen lying there, as well as the burial cloth that had been around Jesus' head. The cloth was folded up by itself, separate from the linen. Finally the other disciple, who had reached the tomb first, also went inside. He saw and believed. (They still did not understand from Scripture that Jesus had to rise from the dead.)

Then the disciples went back to their homes, but Mary stood outside the tomb crying. As she wept, she bent over to look into the tomb and saw two angels in white, seated where Jesus' body had been, one at the head and the other at the foot.

They asked her, "Woman, why are you crying?"

"They have taken my Lord away," she said, "and I don't know where they have put Him." At this, she turned around and saw Jesus standing there, but she did not realize that it was Jesus.

"Woman," He said, "why are you crying? Who is it you are looking for?"

Thinking He was the gardener, she said, "Sir, if you have carried Him away, tell me where you have put Him, and I will get Him."

Jesus said to her, "Mary."

She turned toward Him and cried out in Aramaic, "Rabboni!" (which means Teacher).

Jesus said, "Do not hold on to Me, for I have not yet returned to the Father. Go instead to My brothers and tell them, 'I am returning to My Father and your Father, to My God and your God.' "

Mary Magdalene went to the disciples with the news: "I have seen the Lord!" And she told them that He had said these things to her. John 20:1–18

The Message in Brief

Because the comfort and hope of eternal life relies on the resurrection of Jesus from the dead, it is valuable to investigate all four accounts of that wondrous miracle. When we recognize that these accounts complement rather than contradict each other, we gain greater insight into the nature and purpose of Jesus' ministry.

Working with the Texts

Comparing the Accounts

Read each of the resurrection accounts. Then answer the following questions for each of the accounts.

22

a. Who were the first to appear at the empty tomb on Easter morning?

b. How many angels appeared to the women, and how did they look?

c. What did the angel or angels say to the women?

1. Matthew 28:1–7

a.

b.

c.

2. Mark 16:1–8

a.

b.

c.

3. Luke 24:1–12

a.

b.

c.

4. John 20:1–18

a.

b.

c.

5. Compare the similarities and differences found in each account. Why might these details differ?

Giving Us More Information

1. How do the chief priests and elders in Matthew 28:11–15 attempt to "cover up" the incredible miracle of the resurrection? Look at Mark 2:23–24; Luke 6:6–11; and John 11:45–50 to explain why the religious leaders of Jesus' day felt so threatened by Him. How do these other accounts help us understand the reason for the "cover up"?

2. What were the women's reactions to the resurrection according to Mark 16:8? How does this support one of Mark's themes as described in "Approaching This Study?"

3. Who was the disciple who came to the empty tomb according to Luke 24:12? But who was there according to John 20:3–6? Some might

accuse the writers of contradicting each other. Rather than condemn the accounts as contradictory, can you think of some way to reconcile them?

4. What do Mark 16:4; Luke 24:2; and John 20:1 tell us about the stone which had once blocked the entrance to Jesus' tomb? How does Matthew's account add more detail about the movement of the stone (Matthew 28:2–4)? What does this suggest about the value of having more than one perspective on a single event?

5. What do the details about Jesus' burial linens given in John 20:5–7 suggest to you about Jesus' resurrection? Why would these particular details be appropriate for John's purpose of writing his account as described in John 20:31?

Applying the Message

1. Read Matthew 5:21–26 and list Jesus' commands. If this were the only account of Jesus' teachings, how would you view Him?

2. How would your perception of Him differ or remain the same after reading Mark 10:23–31?

3. Read the parable of the prodigal son in Luke 15:11–32. In this parable, God is represented by the father and sinners are represented by the lost son. How does this parable influence your perception of Jesus, who came to earth to receive the punishment for sin by His death on the cross and reestablish the sin-broken relationship between God and man?

4. Now read the wonderful story of Jesus' first miracle which involved changing water into wine at a wedding feast in Cana (John 2:1–11). What other dimension does this miracle, recorded only in John, add to your view of Jesus?

5. Read Mark 8:27–30. What is your opinion of Jesus?

Taking the Message Home

Review

Read again the different accounts of Jesus' resurrection. Consider the amazing proof God provides as He retells the story through the eyes and words of four different individuals. Then read John 14:19 and take to heart the promise—because of Jesus' resurrection, we can be sure of our own resurrection from the dead.

Looking Ahead

Look up John 14:1–14 and list those statements made by Jesus which you feel need clarification. For example, what does Jesus mean when He says "in My Father's house are many rooms"? And what is Jesus trying to say when He declares, "I am the way and the truth and the life. No one comes to the Father except through Me"? What belief do we gain from the knowledge that "I am in the Father, and the Father is in Me"? Or how about: "I will do whatever you ask in My name, so that the Son may bring glory to the Father. You may ask Me for anything in My name, and I will do it"?

Then find a Bible commentary on John to help clarify what Jesus was saying.

Working Ahead

Choose one or more of the following for individual work:

1. Before the next session, find the following: a commentary on the Bible, a Bible dictionary, and/or a concordance. Look through each of them to learn what "tools" they provide for the student of the Bible. Write down in your own words the purpose of each.

2. Reflect on the saying "Scripture interprets Scripture." At first glance, what does this suggest to you about those areas of the Bible which are difficult to understand?

3. Ask a Christian brother or sister to sit down with you and explain Isaiah 53.

Did you know that a slab of white marble was found in Nazareth around 1878 which says: "Ordinance of Caesar. It is my pleasure that graves and tombs remain undisturbed in perpetuity for those who have made them for the cult of their ancestors, or children, or members of their house ..." The inscription has been dated between 45 and 50 A.D. Many scholars believe it was written as a result of the Christian claim that Jesus had risen from the dead!

Jesus Heals a Leper. From *The Sermon on the Mount* by Cosimo Rosselli (1439–1507), in the Sistine Chapel, Vatican Palace, Rome, Photo by permission of Alinari/Art Resource.

Session 3

Choosing a Gospel Account to Read in Its Entirety

Luke 17:1–19

Approaching This Study

The four Gospels are always interesting. There's always something new to learn from them. They are filled with teachings about God's love and salvation, and they tell us how to live God-pleasing lives. Through Jesus' parables, we learn new and exciting things about God's kingdom. When we realize that all Jesus did and said was for us, then the Bible becomes irresistible. But our growing understanding of the Lord will come to a halt if we don't continually remain in His Word. One of the remarkable things about God's Word is that every time we read it, we discover something fresh. No matter how many times a person reads a portion of Scripture, something new can be applied to her or his life.

To help in our spiritual adventure with the Lord, men and women have developed Bible dictionaries, commentaries, and concordances. These references are not meant to supersede the Word of God. Rather, they point out interesting facets of the Word which we may not have noticed, or they refer us to other portions of Scripture which help us more fully understand the passage we are reading. These references are excellent tools to aid in our spiritual growth.

Bible dictionaries secure more information about something mentioned in a Scripture verse. For example, if one wondered what was meant by "leavened" bread, one could discover how it is made and why it was used by Jesus' contemporaries. Bible commentaries can do this, too, but they also accent connections to other portions of Scripture which may enlighten a particularly difficult passage. Bible concordances help us study the Bible by topic or subject and point us to other places where a particular word is used in Scripture.

The Life of Christ

CHILDHOOD

Birth of Jesus, BETHLEHEM, C. 6/5 B.C., Mt 1:18-25; Lk 2:1-7

Visit by shepherds, BETHLEHEM, Lk 2:8-20

Presentation in the temple, JERUSALEM, Lk 2:21-40

Visit by the Magi, BETHLEHEM, Mt 2:1-12

Escape to Egypt, NILE DELTA, Mt 2:13-18

Return to Nazareth, LOWER GALILEE, Mt 2:19-23

Visit to temple as a boy, JERUSALEM, C. A.D. 7/8, Lk 2:41-52

YEAR OF INAUGURATION

YEAR OF POPULARITY

YEAR OF OPPOSITION

Begin less than full year of ministry

```
10      5              5      10     15     20     25     30     35
||||||||||||||||||||||||||||||||||||||||||||||||||||||||||||||||
         B.C. A.D.
```

Dotted lines leading to the timeline
are meant to define sequence of events only.
Exact dates, even year dates, are generally unknown.

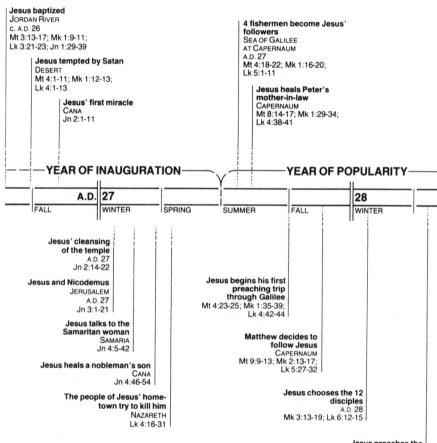

Jesus baptized
JORDAN RIVER
C. A.D. 26
Mt 3:13-17; Mk 1:9-11;
Lk 3:21-23; Jn 1:29-39

**4 fishermen become Jesus'
followers**
SEA OF GALILEE
AT CAPERNAUM
A.D. 27
Mt 4:18-22; Mk 1:16-20;
Lk 5:1-11

Jesus tempted by Satan
DESERT
Mt 4:1-11; Mk 1:12-13;
Lk 4:1-13

**Jesus heals Peter's
mother-in-law**
CAPERNAUM
Mt 8:14-17; Mk 1:29-34;
Lk 4:38-41

Jesus' first miracle
CANA
Jn 2:1-11

YEAR OF INAUGURATION

YEAR OF POPULARITY

A.D. 27

28

FALL   WINTER   SPRING   SUMMER   FALL   WINTER

**Jesus' cleansing
of the temple**
A.D. 27
Jn 2:14-22

Jesus and Nicodemus
JERUSALEM
A.D. 27
Jn 3:1-21

**Jesus begins his first
preaching trip
through Galilee**
Mt 4:23-25; Mk 1:35-39;
Lk 4:42-44

**Jesus talks to the
Samaritan woman**
SAMARIA
Jn 4:5-42

**Matthew decides to
follow Jesus**
CAPERNAUM
Mt 9:9-13; Mk 2:13-17;
Lk 5:27-32

Jesus heals a nobleman's son
CANA
Jn 4:46-54

**Jesus chooses the 12
disciples**
A.D. 28
Mk 3:13-19; Lk 6:12-15

**The people of Jesus' home-
town try to kill him**
NAZARETH
Lk 4:16-31

**Jesus preaches the
"Sermon on the Mount"**
Mt 5:1-7:29; Lk 6:20-49

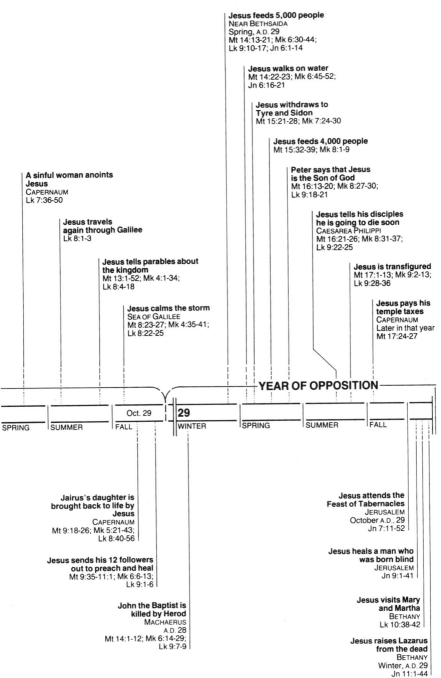

Jesus feeds 5,000 people
NEAR BETHSAIDA
Spring, A.D. 29
Mt 14:13-21; Mk 6:30-44;
Lk 9:10-17; Jn 6:1-14

Jesus walks on water
Mt 14:22-23; Mk 6:45-52;
Jn 6:16-21

**Jesus withdraws to
Tyre and Sidon**
Mt 15:21-28; Mk 7:24-30

Jesus feeds 4,000 people
Mt 15:32-39; Mk 8:1-9

**A sinful woman anoints
Jesus**
CAPERNAUM
Lk 7:36-50

**Peter says that Jesus
is the Son of God**
Mt 16:13-20; Mk 8:27-30;
Lk 9:18-21

**Jesus travels
again through Galilee**
Lk 8:1-3

**Jesus tells his disciples
he is going to die soon**
CAESAREA PHILIPPI
Mt 16:21-26; Mk 8:31-37;
Lk 9:22-25

**Jesus tells parables about
the kingdom**
Mt 13:1-52; Mk 4:1-34;
Lk 8:4-18

Jesus is transfigured
Mt 17:1-13; Mk 9:2-13;
Lk 9:28-36

Jesus calms the storm
SEA OF GALILEE
Mt 8:23-27; Mk 4:35-41;
Lk 8:22-25

**Jesus pays his
temple taxes**
CAPERNAUM
Later in that year
Mt 17:24-27

YEAR OF OPPOSITION

Oct. 29 | **29**

SPRING | SUMMER | FALL | WINTER | SPRING | SUMMER | FALL

**Jairus's daughter is
brought back to life by
Jesus**
CAPERNAUM
Mt 9:18-26; Mk 5:21-43;
Lk 8:40-56

**Jesus attends the
Feast of Tabernacles**
JERUSALEM
October A.D., 29
Jn 7:11-52

**Jesus sends his 12 followers
out to preach and heal**
Mt 9:35-11:1; Mk 6:6-13;
Lk 9:1-6

**Jesus heals a man who
was born blind**
JERUSALEM
Jn 9:1-41

**John the Baptist is
killed by Herod**
MACHAERUS
A.D. 28
Mt 14:1-12; Mk 6:14-29;
Lk 9:7-9

**Jesus visits Mary
and Martha**
BETHANY
Lk 10:38-42

**Jesus raises Lazarus
from the dead**
BETHANY
Winter, A.D. 29
Jn 11:1-44

The Life of Christ (Continued)

The Triumphal Entry, JERUSALEM, Sunday
Mt 21:1-11; Mk 11:1-10; Lk 19:29-44;
Jn 12:12-19

**Jesus begins his last
trip to Jerusalem**
A.D. 30
Lk 17:11

Jesus curses the fig tree
Monday Mt 21:18-19; Mk 11:12-14

Jesus cleanses the temple
Monday Mt 21:12-13; Mk 11:15-18

**Jesus blesses the
little children**
ACROSS THE JORDAN
Mt 19:13-15; Mk 10:13-16;
Lk 18:15-17

The authority of Jesus questioned
Tuesday Mt 21:23-27;
Mk 11:27-33; Lk 20:1-8

Jesus teaches in the temple
Tuesday Mt 21:28-23:39; Mk 12:1-44;
Lk 20:9-21:4

**Jesus talks to the rich
young man**
ACROSS THE JORDAN
Mt 19:16-30; Mk 10:17-31;
Lk 18:18-30

Jesus anointed, BETHANY, Tuesday
Mt 26:6-13; Mk 14:3-9; Jn 12:2-11

The plot against Jesus
Wednesday Mt 26:14-16; Mk 14:10-11;
Lk 22:3-6

**Jesus again tells about
his death and resurrection**
NEAR THE JORDAN
Mt 20:17-19; Mk 10:32-34;
Lk 18:31-34

The Last Supper
Thursday Mt 26:17-29; Mk 14:12-25;
Lk 22:7-20; Jn 13:1-38

Jesus comforts the disciples
Thursday Jn 14:1-16:33

**Jesus heals blind
Bartimaeus**
JERICHO
Mt 20:29-34; Mk 10:46-52;
Lk 18:35-43

Gethsemane, Thursday
Mt 26:36-46; Mk 14:32-42; Lk 22:40-46

Jesus' arrest and trial
Thursday night and Friday
Mt 26:47-27:26; Mk 14:43-15:15;
Lk 22:47-23:25; Jn 18:2-19:16

**Jesus talks to
Zacchaeus**
JERICHO
Lk 19:1-10

Jesus' crucifixion and death, GOLGOTHA,
Friday Mt 27:27-56; Mk 15:16-41;
Lk 23:26-49; Jn 19:17-30

**Jesus returns to Bethany
to visit Mary and Martha**
BETHANY
Jn 11:55-12:1

The burial of Jesus, JOSEPH'S TOMB; Friday
Mt 27:57-66; Mk 15:42-47; Lk 23:50-56;
Jn 19:31-42

30					A.D.	31		
WINTER		SPRING	SUMMER	FALL		WINTER	SPRING	SUMMER

The empty tomb, JERUSALEM, Sunday
Mt 28:1-10; Mk 16:1-8; Lk 24:1-12;
Jn 20:1-10

Mary Magdalene sees Jesus in the
garden, JERUSALEM, Sunday
Mk 16:9-11; Jn 20:11-18

**Jesus appears to the two going to
Emmaus,** Sunday Mk 16:12-13;
Lk 24:13-35

Jesus appears to 10 disciples,
JERUSALEM, Sunday Mk 16:14;
Lk 24:36-43; Jn 20:19-25

Jesus appears to the 11 disciples,
JERUSALEM, One week later
Jn 20:26-31

Jesus talks with some of his disciples,
SEA OF GALILEE, One week later
Jn 21:1-25

**Jesus ascends to his Father in
heaven,** MT OF OLIVES, 40 days later
Mt 28:16-20; Mk 16:19-20; Lk 24:44-53

Dotted lines leading to the timeline
are meant to define sequence of events only.
Exact dates, even year dates, are generally unknown.

An Overview

Read Luke 17:1–19. Notice how the reading incorporates a portion of Jesus' teaching and a demonstration of His miraculous healing.

The Message in Brief

In this short section from Jesus' ministry we are confronted by a number of difficult words, ideas, and actions. As such, it stands as an excellent candidate for the use of our biblical tools: a Bible dictionary, a commentary, and a concordance. By investigating these verses in depth, we can grow in our understanding of Jesus' ministry and its relevance to our lives. We begin to appreciate Luke's perspective on Jesus' ministry.

Working with the Text

A Warning to Tempters (Luke 17:1–3)

1. What does Jesus say about temptations to sin? Can we escape them? *Sin's temptations are bound to come Can't escape them (by our own ability)*

2. Look up "millstone" in a Bible dictionary. What is it? What was it used for? What would happen if a millstone was tied around a person's neck and that person was thrown into the sea? *Heavy stone for grinding grain – large*

3. Look up Luke 17:2 in a Bible commentary and see how it describes "little ones." To whom is Jesus referring when He uses the phrase "little ones"? *children a young in faith*

The Depth of Forgiveness (Luke 17:3–4)

1. Look up these two verses in a commentary. What does it suggest about forgiving someone seven times in a day? Should we take this literally and add up the offenses someone commits so that we can refuse to forgive them on their eighth offense? Look up *seven* in a concordance and read some of the verses it lists. What sense to you get about the use of "seven" in Scripture? *unlimited forgiveness*

"7" used a lot

2. Why would the disciples respond to Jesus' commands by saying, "Increase our faith!" Look up the words in your commentary and suggest what feelings their response reflected.

help to do what Jesus' ect standards for

Faith of a Mustard Seed (Luke 17:6)

1. Look up "mustard seed" in a Bible dictionary. What was its size and what kind of plant would it become? What does this suggest about faith? *thick, tall plant*

2. Look at Matthew 13:31–32 and explain how this passage helps us interpret Luke 17:6. If necessary, use a Bible commentary to help understand the passage in Matthew. *grows strong if cultivated*

A Parable about God's Kingdom (Luke 17:7–10)

A parable is a short, simple story that teaches a lesson about God's kingdom. Consider the parable of the servant and master. What is your impression of the master in this parable? Read an interpretation of this parable in a Bible commentary, then explain how it helps you understand your role in God's kingdom.

parable - earthly story with heavenly meaning
master is demanding - to keep law
unworthy
full reliance on Jesus

The Healing of the 10 Lepers (Luke 17:11–19) *sin-faith-duty*

1. Look up *leprosy* in a Bible dictionary and discuss its implications in Jesus' day. Why would the lepers stand at a distance from Jesus? Why were they together in a "pack" of lepers rather than home with their families?

bacterial disease - highly communicable
went to priests to be declared cleansed and healed
were outcasts — Samaritan was "enemy" of Jesus yet was only one who came back to praise

2. Why would Jesus tell the 10 lepers to go to a priest? Look at your commentary and see if it directs you to Leviticus 13:1–3 or 14:1–32. Read these passages and discuss how they explain Jesus' command.

> The Lord said to Moses and Aaron, "When anyone has a swelling or a rash or a bright spot on his skin that may become an infectious skin disease, he must be brought to Aaron the priest or to one of his sons who is a priest. The priest is to examine the sore on his skin, and if the hair in the sore has turned white and the sore appears to be more than skin deep, it is an infectious skin disease. When the priest examines him, he shall pronounce him ceremonially unclean."(Leviticus 13:2–3)

> The Lord said to Moses,"These are the regulations for the diseased person at the time of his ceremonial cleansing, when he is brought to the priest: The priest is to go outside the camp and examine him. If the person has been healed of his infectious skin disease, the priest shall order that two live clean birds and some cedar wood, scarlet yarn and hyssop be brought for the one to be cleansed. Then the priest shall order that one of the birds be killed over fresh water in a clay pot. He is then to take the live bird and dip it, together with the cedar wood, the scarlet yarn

and the hyssop, into the blood of the bird that was killed over the fresh water. Seven times he shall sprinkle the one to be cleansed of the infectious disease and pronounce him clean. Then he is to release the live bird in the open fields.

"The person to be cleansed must wash his clothes, shave off all his hair and bathe with water; then he will be ceremonially clean. After this he may come into the camp, but he must stay outside his tent for seven days. On the seventh day he must shave off all his hair; he must shave his head, his beard, his eyebrows and the rest of his hair. He must wash his clothes and bathe himself with water, and he will be clean.

"On the eighth day he must bring two male lambs and one ewe lamb a year old, each without defect, along with three-tenths of an ephah of fine flour mixed with oil for a grain offering, and one log of oil. The priest who pronounces him clean shall present both the one to be cleansed and his offerings before the LORD at the entrance to the Tent of Meeting.

"Then the priest is to take one of the male lambs and offer it as a guilt offering, along with the log of oil; he shall wave them before the LORD as a wave offering. He is to slaughter the lamb in the holy place where the sin offering and the burnt offering are slaughtered. Like the sin offering, the guilt offering belongs to the priest; it is most holy. The priest is to take some of the blood of the guilt offering and put it on the lobe of the right ear of the one to be cleansed, on the thumb of his right hand and on the big toe of his right foot. The priest shall then take some of the log of oil, pour it in the palm of his own left hand, dip his right forefinger into the oil in his palm, and with his finger sprinkle some of it before the LORD seven times. The priest is to put some of the oil remaining in his palm on the lobe of the right ear of the one to be cleansed, on the thumb of his right hand and on the big toe of his right foot, on top of the blood of the guilt offering. The rest of the oil in his palm the priest shall put on the head of the one to be cleansed and make atonement for him before the LORD.

"Then the priest is to sacrifice the sin offering and make atonement for the one to be cleansed from his uncleanness. After that, the priest shall slaughter the burnt offering and offer it on the altar, together with the grain offering, and make atonement for him, and he will be clean.

"If, however, he is poor and cannot afford these, he must take one male lamb as a guilt offering to be waved to make atonement for him, together with a tenth of an ephah of fine flour mixed with oil for a grain offering, a log of oil, and two doves or two young pigeons, which he can afford, one for a sin offering and the other for a burnt offering.

"On the eighth day he must bring them for his cleansing to the priest at the entrance to the Tent of Meeting, before the LORD. The priest is to take the lamb for the guilt offering, together with the log of oil, and wave them before the LORD as a wave offering. He shall slaughter the lamb for the guilt offering and take some of its blood and put it on the lobe of the right ear of the one to be cleansed, on the thumb of his right hand and on the big toe of his right foot. The priest is to pour some of the oil into the palm of his own left hand, and with his right forefinger sprinkle some of the oil from his palm seven times before the LORD. Some of the oil in his palm he is to put on the same places he put the blood of the guilt offering—on the lobe of the right ear of the one to be cleansed, on the thumb of his right hand and on the big toe of his right foot. The rest of the oil in his palm the priest shall put on the head of the one to be cleansed, to make atonement for him before the LORD. Then he shall sacrifice the doves or the young pigeons, which the person can afford, one as a sin offering and the other as a burnt offering, together with the grain offering. In this way the priest will make atonement before the LORD on behalf of the one to be cleansed."

These are the regulations for anyone who has an infectious skin disease and who cannot afford the regular offerings for his cleansing. Leviticus 14:1–32

3. Look up *Samaritan* in a Bible dictionary. Who were they and why would Luke be so interested in describing one leper as such? What does this say about the faith and gratitude of those we might write off as "inferior"? active hatred

4. Who does Jesus claim to be in Luke 17:18? Look up *blasphemy* in your Bible dictionary and explain how it is defined and what punishment it deserved. How does this help explain the hostility many religious rulers held for Jesus?

Applying the Message

1. One fundamental way of interpreting Jesus' sayings in the four gospels is to categorize them as either "Law" or "Gospel." The Law involves how God commands us to live. "Gospel" refers to God's forgiveness through Jesus' death on the cross for our failure to keep God's command. Look again at Luke 17:1–4. Determine which sayings are "Law." Gospel, although not implicit in these verses, is definitely evident in the unlimited forgiveness Jesus offers to all sinners. How is "Gospel" also implied?

2. Read Romans 10:17. How does this verse help us understand how faith can "increase" even as the disciples wished? How can we be assured that the Word will rule in our hearts and minds according to Colossians 3:16? What does this suggest about the importance of reading God's Word and hearing it in worship?

> Consequently, faith comes from hearing the message, and the message is heard through the word of Christ. Romans 10:17

> Let the word of Christ dwell in you richly as you teach and admonish one another with all wisdom, and as you sing psalms, hymns and spiritual songs with gratitude in your hearts to God. Colossians 3:16

3. When you read the parable of the master and the servant in Luke 17:7–10, what does it suggest about fulfilling God's expectations? About a self-righteous attitude about our goodness?

4. Interestingly, the healing of the 10 lepers is only recorded in the gospel of Luke. One of Luke's themes is that Jesus is a God of grace and forgiveness for *all* people. How does this story emphasize that theme?

5. As you spend time reading the gospels, one may become your favorite. That doesn't mean you will neglect the others, but one Gospel account may appeal to you more than the others.

a. Look up Matthew 8:14–17. How does Matthew interpret Jesus' miracle as a fulfillment of Scripture?

b. Look up Mark 7:31–37. How does Mark demonstrate Jesus' "amazing" miracle?

c. Look up Luke 13:11–13. How does Luke demonstrate Jesus' miracles as a gift to *all* people?

d. And look up John 11:17–24. How does John emphasize Jesus' miracle as a sign that He is the Son of God?

e. Which Gospel perspective of a miracle appeals most to you? Why? Read the Gospel that appeals most to you from beginning to end.

Taking the Message Home

Review

Read again Luke 17:1–19 and think about all those things in the verses which demonstrate Jesus' compassion and forgiveness. Pray that you will be able to forgive others even as Jesus has forgiven you.

If you were not able to read Isaiah 53 after the last session, do so now.

Use your biblical "tools" to help you understand how this prophecy directs us to Jesus.

Looking Ahead

Read Acts 1:1–11. When we start reading the book of Acts, we begin at the end of Jesus' ministry. Acts gives us a fascinating account of what happened to God's people immediately following Jesus' ascension. Reflect on how important it was for the Holy Spirit to empower the disciples and ignite the spread of Jesus' love and forgiveness throughout the world.

Working Ahead

Before the next session, consider doing one or more of the following:

1. Look up *witness* in a dictionary and write down some ways believers in Christ can "witness" to Him. When we "witness" to our Lord, must it always be done with words? What role do our actions play in sharing the message of Jesus? What reactions might we expect from our witness?

2. Ask your church's "record keeper" whether he or she has a brief history of your congregation. If you can get a copy, read what joys and sorrows the church has endured. Discover its important historical dates and the names of its pastors. Find out which pastor served the longest and which the shortest.

3. Look again at Acts 1:1–2 and Luke 1:1–4. Whose name connects the two writings? What does this suggest about the author of Luke and Acts? Using your commentary, find out the significance of the phrase *most excellent Theophilus*.

4. Ask a Christian brother or sister if he or she has ever been "persecuted" for the faith. What happened? How did it feel? Did it make her/him less inclined to follow the Lord? Why or why not? Bring these recollections to the next session for sharing.

Did you know that the Bible describes Jesus performing at least 35 miracles—17 of them involve bodily cures, 9 are miracles over nature, 6 are exorcisms, and 3 are resurrections from the dead. The Bible says Jesus performed many other miracles as well, but only these 35 are described in some detail.

Paul's Missionary Journeys

In four long journeys Paul brought the Gospel to the Roman Empire and established a strong network of Christian churches. His first journey (A.D. 46–48) was to Cyprus and Asia Minor, where he often encountered hostility from the Jews. Undaunted, he returned on a second visit. Then he continued to Macedonia and westward, establishing a major church at Corinth (49–52). On another journey (53–57), Paul set up a church at Ephesus. A voyage to western Europe was prevented in 57 by his arrest in Jerusalem and by his subsequent imprisonment in Rome.

Session 4

The Spirit's Transforming Power

Acts 9:1–22

Approaching This Study

All four gospels conclude at the end of Jesus' ministry. And in many ways each ending leaves the impression that there must be something more to the story. The gospels tell us about Jesus' life, death, resurrection, and ascension. But after Jesus ascends into heaven, the reader is curious about the continuing role of the disciples. What happened to them after their profound experience with the Lord? What did they do next?

The book of Acts is so important because it shows the tremendous impact Jesus had on the lives of His followers. It demonstrates how Jesus sent His Holy Spirit, as He promised to His followers, inspiring them to confess boldly His person and work throughout the world. As a result, some of them were imprisoned or killed. Some were stoned to death, and all of them had to endure hatred and scorn. Although they may at times have become discouraged, they never surrendered to the opposition. After Jesus' ascension, they worked harder than ever.

Before Jesus' ascension, the disciples of the Lord were reluctant witnesses. Afterwards, they were unstoppable in their testimony of faith. The book of Acts shows how radically the disciples were transformed by the Holy Spirit to become the pillars of the early Christian church. The Spirit gave them great power and strength.

According to Jesus' promises, how would the disciples receive this transforming power? Look up John 15:26–27 and Luke 24:49. Then describe Jesus' promises.

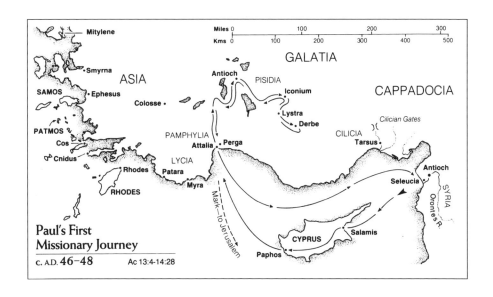

Paul's First
Missionary Journey

c. A.D. 46–48   Ac 13:4-14:28

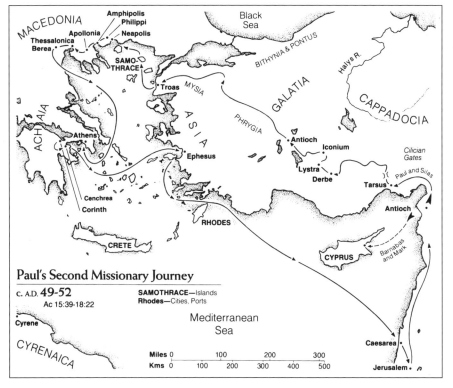

Paul's Second Missionary Journey

c. A.D. 49-52   SAMOTHRACE—Islands
Ac 15:39-18:22   Rhodes—Cities, Ports

Maps taken from NIV STUDY BIBLE. Copyright © 1985 by the Zondervan Corporation. Used by permission of Zondervan Publishing House.

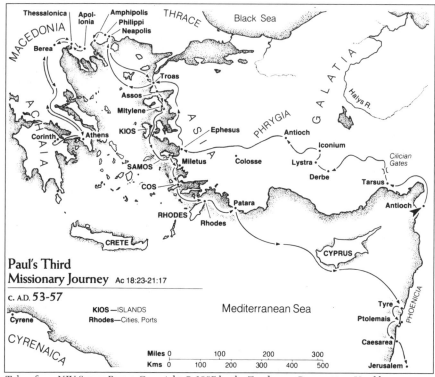

Paul's Third
Missionary Journey Ac 18:23-21:17

c. A.D. 53-57

KIOS—ISLANDS
Rhodes—Cities, Ports

Mediterranean Sea

Miles 0   100   200   300
Kms 0 100 200 300 400 500

Taken from NIV STUDY BIBLE. Copyright © 1985 by the Zondervan Corporation. Used by permission of Zondervan Publishing House.

An Overview

Read Acts 9:1–22. Jesus converted Saul, who was a Pharisee and who hated the Christians, on the road to Damascus. His conversion changed his entire life. After his conversion, he used his Roman (Gentile) name, Paul. As you read about Saul/Paul's transformation, consider the moment when God called you to be His own.

The Message in Brief

The book of Acts is a record of the Holy Spirit's transforming power. Through the Holy Spirit, people were transformed into "spiritual warriors," determined to spread Jesus' message of salvation even if it cost them their lives. Many of them, Jewish by birth, had to fight the false ideas of their own people. Their church leaders tried to force them not to preach about Jesus Christ. Government officials often treated them as rabble-rousers. Paul's miraculous conversion is but one example of such a "transformation," and, as such, stands as a model of the trans-forming power of the Holy Spirit witnessed in the book of Acts.

Working with the Text

Saul's Murderous Attitude (Acts 9:1–2)

1. In Acts 8:1–3 and 9:1–2 we read about Saul's attacks against the early Christians. One day, he decided to go to Damascus. What attitude did Saul have towards the followers of Christ according to verse 9:1? What was his purpose in going to Damascus?

2. The followers of Christ encountered various responses to their message of salvation in Jesus Christ. Look up the following verses and describe the reactions of those who heard about Jesus:

a. Acts 2:1–13

b. Acts 4:1–4

c. Acts 5:12–20

d. Acts 7:54–8:1

Saul's Miraculous Transformation (Acts 9:3–19)

1. Saul's conversion was truly a miraculous event. It's only natural that he should describe this event several times. Look up Acts 22:6–16 and Acts 26:12–18 and compare his accounts. What additional facts do we learn about Saul's conversion?

2. Saul was not the only one in Acts to be transformed by the power of the Holy Spirit. Read each of the following passages and describe the personal transformations that took place:

a. Acts 8: 26–39

b. Acts 10:9–28

c. Acts 16:22–34

d. Acts 19:1–7

3. The book of Acts has sometimes been called "The Acts of the Holy Spirit." Why is that? See Acts 1:4–5; 2:1–4; 4:8–12; 10:44–48; and 13:49–52.

The Power of Discipleship (Acts 9:19–22)

1. After Saul's conversion, he was empowered by God's Spirit to deliver the Word of God throughout the world. In these verses, what evidence of the Spirit's work do you see in Saul/Paul?

2. Compare Peter's attitude in Matthew 26:69–75 with his speech of Acts 4:1–13. Explain the difference in Peter's attitude.

> Now Peter was sitting out in the courtyard, and a servant girl came to him. "You also were with Jesus of Galilee," she said.
>
> But he denied it before them all. "I don't know what you're talking about," he said.
>
> Then he went out to the gateway, where another girl saw him and said to the people there, "This fellow was with Jesus of Nazareth."
>
> He denied it again, with an oath: "I don't know the man!"
>
> After a little while, those standing there went up to Peter and said, "Surely you are one of them, for your accent gives you away."
>
> Then he began to call down curses on himself and he swore to them, "I don't know the man!"
>
> Immediately a rooster crowed. Then Peter remembered the word Jesus had spoken: "Before the rooster crows, you will disown Me three times." And he went outside and wept bitterly. Matthew 26:69–75

3. What other power did the disciples receive besides the courage to preach God's Word? Suggest some miraculous gifts given to the apostles according to Acts 3:1–9; 5:12–16; 8:4–7; and 9:32–42.

4. There were some who wanted the power of the Spirit for selfish reasons (Acts 8:18–25). How much do you think people today would pay for the gift of healing demonstrated by these early disciples?

5. Read Acts 15:1–21. What momentous decision did the disciples have to make at the Jerusalem Council? Explain how they came to their decision and the significance of their decision.

6. How would you describe the importance of the Spirit's power in strengthening Paul according to 2 Corinthians 11:22–29?

Are they Hebrews? So am I. Are they Israelites? So am I. Are they Abraham's descendants? So am I. Are they servants of Christ? (I am out of my mind to talk like this.) I am more. I have worked much harder, been in prison more frequently, been flogged more severely, and been exposed to death again and again. Five times I received from the Jews the forty lashes minus one. Three times I was beaten with rods, once I was stoned, three times I was shipwrecked, I spent a night and a day in the open sea, I have been constantly on the move. I have been in danger from rivers, in danger from bandits, in danger from my own countrymen, in danger from Gentiles; in danger in the city, in danger in the country, in danger at sea; and in danger from false brothers. I have labored and toiled and have often gone without sleep; I have known hunger and thirst and have often gone without food; I have been cold and naked. Besides everything else, I face daily the pressure of my concern for all the churches. Who is weak, and I do not feel weak? Who is led into sin, and I do not inwardly burn? 2 Corinthians 11:22–29

Applying the Message

1. Read Acts 1:1–11. What do you think it means to be a witness to Christ? How are you a witness?

2. How do you know whether the Holy Spirit dwells in your heart and mind? The Bible gives us some indicators of His presence. Read the following Bible passages and suggest what kind of signs suggest that the Spirit of the Lord dwells in a person.

a. But the fruit of the Spirit is love, joy, peace, patience, kindness, goodness, faithfulness, gentleness and self-control. Against such things there is no law. Galatians 5:22–23

b. He saved us, not because of righteous things we had done, but because of His mercy. He saved us through the washing of rebirth and renewal by the Holy Spirit, whom He poured out on us generously through Jesus Christ our Savior. Titus 3:5–6

c. Therefore I tell you that no one who is speaking by the Spirit of God says, "Jesus be cursed," and no one can say, "Jesus is Lord," except by the Holy Spirit. 1 Corinthians 12:3

d. Do not get drunk on wine, which leads to debauchery. Instead, be filled with the Spirit. Speak to one another with psalms, hymns and spiritual songs. Sing and make music in your heart to the Lord, always giving thanks to God the Father for everything, in the name of our Lord Jesus Christ. Ephesians 5:18–20

3. Do you think you could tolerate the kind of persecution experienced by the early Christians? Why? Why do you think God allows Christians to be persecuted for their faith?

4. We are certainly impressed by how the Spirit of the Lord empowered the early disciples. We can also praise God for the Spirit's empowerment of Christians throughout history, including men like John Hus, William Tyndale, Martin Luther, and C. F. W. Walther. But does He still empower people today? How does He affect them? Look at Romans 1:16, Ephesians 1:18–21; 3:7, 20–21; and Colossians 1:29. Explain your answer.

> I am not ashamed of the gospel, because it is the power of God for the salvation of everyone who believes: first for the Jew, then for the Gentile. Romans 1:16

> I pray also that the eyes of your heart may be enlightened in order that you may know the hope to which He has called you, the riches of His glorious inheritance in the saints, and His incomparably great power for us who believe. That power is like the working of His mighty strength, which He exerted in Christ when He raised Him from the dead and seated Him at His right hand in the heavenly realms, far above all rule and authority, power and dominion, and every title that can be given, not only in the present age but also in the one to come. Ephesians 1:18–21

> I became a servant of this gospel by the gift of God's grace given me through the working of His power. Ephesians 3:7

> Now to Him who is able to do immeasurably more than all we ask or imagine, according to His power that is at work within us, to Him be glory in the church and in Christ Jesus throughout all generations, for ever and ever! Amen. Ephesians 3:20–21

To this end I labor, struggling with all His energy, which so power-fully works in me. Colossians 1:29

5. When we read the book of Acts, we are awed by the miraculous powers demonstrated by the Spirit. The disciples brought the message of the Gospel in different languages. The sick were healed. The disturbed were restored. These miracles continue today, but they are most frequently displayed through the tools God has given us. How do the following demonstrate God's work to effect the same kind of outcomes today?

a. A missionary spends four years learning Japanese before beginning His ministry.

b. A doctor uses the latest technological breakthroughs to locate a small, cancerous tumor. Then, through modern medicine, the tumor is treated and destroyed.

c. The Bible is translated into braille so that the blind throughout the nation can read it.

d. A schizophrenic who has been hearing demonic "voices" is given an experimental drug which allows him to get through the day without hearing things.

Taking the Message Home

Review

Read Acts 28:23–31. The apostle Paul is under house arrest in Rome, waiting to be put on trial for his ministry. While he waits, Paul invites the leaders of the Jews to hear him speak about Jesus Christ. In what ways do these last verses of Acts summarize the book as a whole?

Looking Ahead

Romans 3:9–31 is a good link between the conclusion of Acts and the beginning of Paul's letters. Read this section and determine which verses speak of "Law," that is, God's demands of us, and which speak of "Gospel," that is, the good news of forgiveness and salvation through Jesus Christ. What is happening to the Word as it applies to Jew and Gentile? Who is rejecting it and who is receiving it?

Working Ahead

Choose one or more of the following suggestions for further study:

1. Consider the last letter you wrote. Where did you place your greeting? What words did you use to close your letter? Where did you sign your name? Did you put a date on it? Bring these thoughts to the next session as we consider the format of Paul's letters.

2. Look up *angel* in your Bible dictionary and be prepared to discuss their role in God's kingdom.

3. Consider the scriptural teaching, we are "saved by grace through faith." Contemplate why we say we are saved "by grace" and not "by faith."

Did you know that when Saul began his persecution of the Christian church, it caused a dispersion of Christians into all the Roman world. Saul thought he could exterminate this "new" religion, but through the providence of God, the persecuted fled Jerusalem and carried the Gospel message throughout the Roman Empire. This is but one example of God transforming that which appeared to be tragic into something wonderful.

The Appian Way, over which Paul passed on his way into Rome
(Acts 28:15). Photo by permission of Alinari/Art Resource.

Session 5

Romans and Galatians: the Gift of Salvation

Romans 3:9–31, Galatians 3

Approaching This Study

There are many reasons to write letters. Sometimes they express our love and care for someone. Sometimes they can be angry and blunt. We write letters which may be very personal, and we write letters which simply "get down to business." What kind of letter was the last one you wrote?

Most of the New Testament books consist of letters which were written to Christian congregations or individuals. Each letter covers different topics. When we read them we gain a better understanding of the person and work of Jesus on our behalf and God's will for those whom He has redeemed by His grace alone through faith. These letters are called *epistles,* and they discuss topics such as life, death, judgment, heaven, forgiveness, and sin. The New Testament letters were written by Paul, Peter, James, John, and Jude.

The first time you read these epistles, they may seem difficult to understand. But the more you study and grow in them, the easier they become. Most of the letters are very short. One can read most of them in 20 or 30 minutes, making them excellent tools for daily study and devotion.

When Paul writes letters, he names himself and those to whom the letter is addressed first. Then he blesses his readers. At the end of the letter, he frequently sends greetings to his friends. How does this compare to the structure of your letters?

In this session we will be considering Romans and Galatians. The first letter was written to the Christian congregation in Rome. The other was written to a number of congregations in the province of Galatia. Galatians is called a "circular letter" because after reading it one congregation would deliver the letter to another. "Circular letters" may seem less personal because they address a number of different congregations. The letters to Rome and the churches in Galatia are similar in their emphasis on salvation by grace alone through faith alone in Christ Jesus.

Timeline of Paul's Life

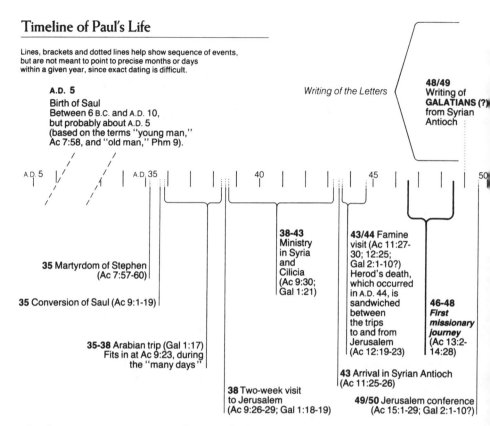

Lines, brackets and dotted lines help show sequence of events, but are not meant to point to precise months or days within a given year, since exact dating is difficult.

A.D. 5
Birth of Saul
Between 6 B.C. and A.D. 10, but probably about A.D. 5 (based on the terms "young man," Ac 7:58, and "old man," Phm 9).

Writing of the Letters

48/49
Writing of
GALATIANS (?)
from Syrian
Antioch

A.D. 5   A.D. 35   40   45   50

35 Martyrdom of Stephen (Ac 7:57-60)

35 Conversion of Saul (Ac 9:1-19)

35-38 Arabian trip (Gal 1:17) Fits in at Ac 9:23, during the "many days"

38-43
Ministry in Syria and Cilicia (Ac 9:30; Gal 1:21)

38 Two-week visit to Jerusalem (Ac 9:26-29; Gal 1:18-19)

43/44 Famine visit (Ac 11:27-30; 12:25; Gal 2:1-10?) Herod's death, which occurred in A.D. 44, is sandwiched between the trips to and from Jerusalem (Ac 12:19-23)

43 Arrival in Syrian Antioch (Ac 11:25-26)

46-48
First missionary journey (Ac 13:2-14:28)

49/50 Jerusalem conference (Ac 15:1-29; Gal 2:1-10?)

Taken from NIV STUDY BIBLE. Copyright © 1985 by the Zondervan Corporation. Used by permission of Zondervan Publishing House.

An Overview

Read Romans 3:9–31 and Galatians 3:1–29 and consider the similar themes evident in both letters.

The Message in Brief

Through these two letters we gain a deeper understanding of the role of God's Law and the depth of His Good News—Gospel—of forgiveness and grace. We are taught the function of faith in the divine plan of salvation. Romans and Galatians give us a clear picture of the grace of God which works through faith in order to redeem and restore sinful people. These two letters were the most important source of Martin Luther's discovery that we are saved "by grace through faith in Jesus Christ."

56

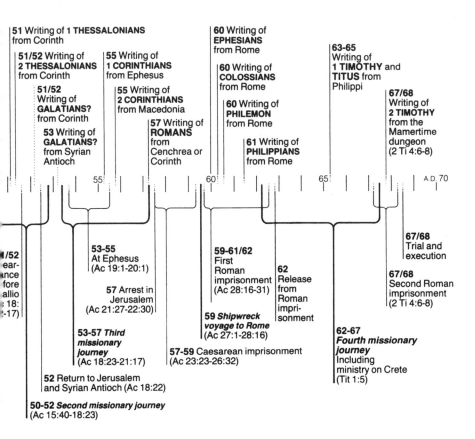

51 Writing of 1 THESSALONIANS from Corinth

51/52 Writing of 2 THESSALONIANS from Corinth

51/52 Writing of GALATIANS? from Corinth

53 Writing of GALATIANS? from Syrian Antioch

55 Writing of 1 CORINTHIANS from Ephesus

55 Writing of 2 CORINTHIANS from Macedonia

57 Writing of ROMANS from Cenchrea or Corinth

60 Writing of EPHESIANS from Rome

60 Writing of COLOSSIANS from Rome

60 Writing of PHILEMON from Rome

61 Writing of PHILIPPIANS from Rome

63-65 Writing of 1 TIMOTHY and TITUS from Philippi

67/68 Writing of 2 TIMOTHY from the Mamertime dungeon (2 Ti 4:6-8)

55   60   65   A.D. 70

/52 ear- nce fore allio 18: -17)

53-55 At Ephesus (Ac 19:1-20:1)

57 Arrest in Jerusalem (Ac 21:27-22:30)

53-57 *Third missionary journey* (Ac 18:23-21:17)

52 Return to Jerusalem and Syrian Antioch (Ac 18:22)

50-52 *Second missionary journey* (Ac 15:40-18:23)

59-61/62 First Roman imprisonment (Ac 28:16-31)

62 Release from Roman impri- sonment

59 *Shipwreck voyage to Rome* (Ac 27:1-28:16)

57-59 Caesarean imprisonment (Ac 23:23-26:32)

62-67 *Fourth missionary journey* Including ministry on Crete (Tit 1:5)

67/68 Trial and execution

67/68 Second Roman imprisonment (2 Ti 4:6-8)

Working with the Text

Sin and the Law

1. When Paul declares that both Jews and Gentiles are sinners, he quotes various verses from the Psalms. As you read these quotations in Romans 3:10–18 consider: Who is naturally righteous or, "good," in God's eyes? What is our value to God under the Law? How do the quoted verses indicate that our sinful state leads to sinful actions?

2. According to Romans 3:19–20 what is one purpose of God's Law? How is this purpose evident in many of Jesus' words from the Sermon on the Mount, particularly Matthew 5:19–20, 21–22, 27–28, 32, 34–37, and 38–42? How do Jesus' words underscore the reality that no one can be righteous or "good" before God by their own efforts? How does James 2:10–11 and Leviticus 19:2 support this truth?

"Anyone who breaks one of the least of these commandments and teaches others to do the same will be called least in the kingdom of heaven, but whoever practices and teaches these commands will be called great in the kingdom of heaven. For I tell you that unless your righteousness surpasses that of the Pharisees and the teachers of the law, you will certainly not enter the kingdom of heaven." Matthew 5:19–20

"You have heard that it was said to the people long ago, 'Do not murder, and anyone who murders will be subject to judgment.' But I tell you that anyone who is angry with his brother will be subject to judgment. Again, anyone who says to his brother, 'Raca,' is answerable to the Sanhedrin. But anyone who says, 'You fool!' will be in danger of the fire of hell." Matthew 5:21–22

"You have heard that it was said, 'Do not commit adultery.' But I tell you that anyone who looks at a woman lustfully has already committed adultery with her in his heart." Matthew 5:27–28

"But I tell you that anyone who divorces his wife, except for marital unfaithfulness, causes her to become an adulteress, and anyone who marries the divorced woman commits adultery." Matthew 5:32

"But I tell you, Do not swear at all: either by heaven, for it is God's throne; or by the earth, for it is His footstool; or by Jerusalem, for it is the city of the Great King. And do not swear by your head, for you cannot make even one hair white or black. Simply let your 'Yes' be 'Yes,' and your 'No,' 'No'; anything beyond this comes from the evil one." Matthew 5:34–37

"You have heard that it was said, 'Eye for eye, and tooth for tooth.' But I tell you, Do not resist an evil person. If someone strikes you on the right cheek, turn to him the other also. And if someone wants to sue you and take your tunic, let him have your cloak as well. If someone forces you to go one mile, go with him two miles. Give to the one who asks you, and do not turn away from the one who wants to borrow from you." Matthew 5:38–42

"For whoever keeps the whole law and yet stumbles at just one point is guilty of breaking all of it. For He who said, "Do not commit adultery," also said, "Do not murder." If you do not commit adultery but do commit murder, you have become a lawbreaker. James 2:10–11

"Speak to the entire assembly of Israel and say to them: 'Be holy because I, the LORD Your God, am holy'." Leviticus 19:2

3. Read Galatians 3:3–5. What false doctrine had arisen among the churches in Galatia to cause Paul to write?

4. What does Paul say in Galatians 3:10–11 about those who attempt to live by the Law? How does this compare with what Paul wrote in Romans 3:10–18?

The Gospel of Grace

1. Read Romans 3:21–24. Who gives us righteousness, or goodness? How did He bring us that goodness according to verses 24–25? Explain how Galatians 3:13 describes this same process.

2. God's method for declaring us righteous is expressed most succinctly in 2 Corinthians 5:21. After reading this verse, explain in your own words how God gave us His righteousness.

God made Him who had no sin to be sin for us, so that in Him we might become the righteousness of God. 2 Corinthians 5:21

Grace Received through Faith

1. We now know where righteousness comes from. But through what means does God give us this righteousness according to Galatians 3:14, 22 and Romans 3:22?

2. How does the author of Hebrews 11:1 define faith? How do we use "faith" when we consider the creation of the universe according to 11:3? How did many Old Testament figures find their salvation by God's grace through faith? (See Hebrews 11:4, 5, 7, 17, 20, 21, 22, and 32–34). Even though Jesus Christ had not yet ministered on earth, what kind of "faith" did these Old Testament people demonstrate according to Hebrews 11:13–16?

Now faith is being sure of what we hope for and certain of what we do not see. Hebrews 11:1

By faith we understand that the universe was formed at God's command, so that what is seen was not made out of what was visible. Hebrews 11:3

By faith Abel offered God a better sacrifice than Cain did. By faith he was commended as a righteous man, when God spoke well of his offerings. And by faith he still speaks, even though he is dead. Hebrews 11:4

By faith Enoch was taken from this life, so that he did not experience death; he could not be found, because God had taken him away. For before he was taken, he was commended as one who pleased God. Hebrews 11:5

By faith Noah, when warned about things not yet seen, in holy fear built an ark to save his family. By his faith he condemned the world and became heir of the righteousness that comes by faith. Hebrews 11:7

By faith Abraham, when God tested him, offered Isaac as a sacrifice. He who had received the promises was about to sacrifice his one and only son. Hebrews 11:17

By faith Isaac blessed Jacob and Esau in regard to their future. Hebrews 11:20

By faith Jacob, when he was dying, blessed each of Joseph's sons, and worshiped as he leaned on the top of his staff. Hebrews 11:21

By faith Joseph, when his end was near, spoke about the exodus of the Israelites from Egypt and gave instructions about his bones. Hebrews 11:22

And what more shall I say? I do not have time to tell about Gideon, Barak, Samson, Jephthah, David, Samuel and the prophets, who through faith conquered kingdoms, administered justice, and gained what was promised; who shut the mouths of lions, quenched the fury of the flames, and escaped the edge of the sword; whose weakness was turned to strength; and who became powerful in battle and routed foreign armies. Hebrews 11:32–34

All these people were still living by faith when they died. They did not receive the things promised; they only saw them and welcomed them from a distance. And they admitted that they were aliens and strangers on earth. People who say such things show that they are looking for a country of their own. If they had been thinking of the country they had left, they would have had opportunity to return. Instead, they were longing for a better country—a heavenly one. Therefore God is not ashamed to be called their God, for He has prepared a city for them. Hebrews 11:13–16

3. Can we take credit for the faith we possess? Consider what Paul says in Romans 3:27, then see how Paul underscores the source of faith in Ephesians 2:8–9. From where does Paul say faith comes?

For it is by grace you have been saved, through faith—and this not from yourselves, it is the gift of God—not by works, so that no one can boast. Ephesians 2:8–9

The Purpose of the Law for Christians

1. The question naturally arises, "If we are saved by grace through faith, why care anymore about the Law?" Since we can't live the Law perfectly, and we are forgiven anyway by the grace of God through faith in the death and resurrection of Jesus Christ, why not break every law in the book and enjoy ourselves while we can? How does Paul answer this perfectly logical question in Romans 3:31 and 6:1–2, 11–14?

2. Paul underscores the ongoing need for the Law in Colossians 3:1–11. What does he have to say about the way followers of Christ demonstrate their faith?

> Since, then, you have been raised with Christ, set your hearts on things above, where Christ is seated at the right hand of God. Set your minds on things above, not on earthly things. For you died, and your life is now hidden with Christ in God. When Christ, who is your life, appears, then you also will appear with Him in glory.
>
> Put to death, therefore, whatever belongs to your earthly nature: sexual immorality, impurity, lust, evil desires and greed, which is idolatry. Because of these, the wrath of God is coming. You used to walk in these ways, in the life you once lived. But now you must rid yourselves of all such things as these: anger, rage, malice, slander, and filthy language from your lips. Do not lie to each other, since you have taken off your old self with its practices and have put on the new self, which is being renewed in knowledge in the image of its Creator. Here there is no Greek or Jew, circumcised or uncircumcised, barbarian, Scythian, slave or free, but Christ is all, and is in all. Colossians 3:1–11

3. Is God's Law, then, something that forces us to live dispirited, regimented, and glum lives? Or is God's Law a gift which teaches us how to live the most joyful and fulfilling life possible in a fallen world? What does Psalm 19:7–11 and Psalm 119:172–175 suggest?

> The law of the LORD is perfect,
>   reviving the soul.
> The statutes of the LORD are trustworthy,
>   making wise the simple.

The precepts of the LORD are right,
>giving joy to the heart.
The commands of the LORD are radiant,
>giving light to the eyes.
The fear of the LORD is pure,
>enduring forever.
The ordinances of the LORD are sure
>and altogether righteous.
They are more precious than gold,
>than much pure gold;
they are sweeter than honey,
>than honey from the comb.
By them is your servant warned;
>in keeping them there is great reward.
>>Psalm 19:7–11

May my tongue sing of Your word,
>for all Your commands are righteous.
May Your hand be ready to help me,
>for I have chosen Your precepts.
I long for Your salvation, O LORD,
>and Your law is my delight.
Let me live that I may praise You,
>and may Your laws sustain me.
>>Psalm 119:172–175

Applying the Message

1. What would you do if you were afflicted with cancer right now, but had no idea of its presence? Would it make any difference in the way you lived or behaved? Why?

2. Suppose tomorrow you looked in the mirror and discovered its devastation raging throughout your body. How would you feel? What would it force you to do?

3. What would the doctor do to heal you of this dreaded, life-threatening disease?

4. The doctor announces you have been healed. Through all the discoveries of modern medicine, the illness has been defeated. How would you feel toward the doctor? Would you begrudgingly pay your bill or be happy to pay because of his healing work?

5. Through the questions above we have created a familiar illustration for understanding God's plan and process of salvation. Consider that sin is represented by the cancer, the doctor represents Jesus Christ, and the medicines and technology represent the faith God gives us. If we didn't know we were sinners, would we care? How does the Law "diagnose" us according to Romans 7:7? What is the consequence of sin according to Romans 6:23?

6. Realizing we have a deadly "disease" called sin, whom should that knowledge force us to seek? Why? Once again, see Romans 6:23.

7. What's the medicine Jesus gives us to heal us? Look up Galatians 2:15–16.

8. What is our attitude toward the God who "heals" us of sin according to Galatians 5:22–26?

9. Look at Jesus' simple words in John 3:16–18. How does Jesus summarize everything we've talked about in this session?

> "For God so loved the world that He gave His one and only Son, that whoever believes in Him shall not perish but have eternal life. For God did not send His Son into the world to condemn the world, but to save the world through Him. Whoever believes in Him is not condemned, but whoever does not believe stands condemned already because he has not believed in the name of God's one and only Son."

10. How does the gift of salvation defined by Paul in his letters to the Roman and the Galatian congregations change or support your perspective of receiving eternal life?

Taking the Message Home

Review

Read again the verses from this session. Then write down in your own words how Romans and Galatians depict the "process of salvation." Be prepared to share your understanding with other participants during the next session.

Looking Ahead

Read Ephesians 2:11–22 and reflect on how one becomes a member of the church. Is genuine church membership a matter of us choosing God or God choosing us? Is it correct to think we have the power to join the church or quit it any time we want to?

Working Ahead

Choose one or more of the following suggestions for additional work before the next session:

1. Write down all those things you like best about your church. Be prepared to share them during the next session.

2. Reflect on your view of different roles within the family. Should father, mother, and children fulfill different functions within the family? What should they be and why? How do you think such roles have changed over the last decades?

Did you know that the first Jewish merchants and artisans settled in the city of Rome as early as the third century before Christ's birth. By the time of Jesus' birth, there were more than 8,000 Jews present in the city. Although many were expelled from Rome for a period of time, the Jews introduced an understanding of only one God, rather than the plethora of gods worshiped by the Romans. As a result of Jewish influence, Rome was better prepared to hear the message that Jesus was "God made man" who came to sacrifice Himself for the sins of the world.

The temple of Hadrian at Ephesus, capital of the Roman province of Asia, where Christianity triumphed over the worship of Diana. Photo by permission of SEF/Art Resource.

Session 6

Ephesians and Colossians: Lessons about the Church

Ephesians 2; Colossians 3:1–17

Approaching This Study

It is likely Paul wrote his letters to the Ephesians and Colossians during the same year, probably around the year 60. Both letters teach similar lessons about the church, describing what the church is and what membership in the church is all about.

Ephesus and Colosse were located in what we call western Turkey today. Both cities enjoyed commerce and trade. Ephesus rested on the coast of the Aegean Sea and Colosse lay inland somewhat, but on a great trade route from Ephesus to the lands of the east. By the time of Paul's writings, Colosse was quickly fading in economic importance. Maybe that's why Paul used Ephesus rather than Colosse as his center of outreach for three years.

Paul's letters, inspired by the Holy Spirit, indicate that the church is "the body of Christ." What does that mean? It suggests that the members of the church are not only bonded with one another as parts of a "body" working together for the common good, but they are also subservient to their "Head," which is the Lord (see Ephesians 4:15–16). Paul explains that following the will of God does not simply involve worshiping the Lord by oneself. It involves working and worshiping together with other members of the congregation.

Most congregations have members who rarely attend worship, never contribute to the work of the church, and ignore involvement in church activities. Although they may be listed on the congregation's official "roster," one questions whether they are still authentic church members. There is no doubt, according to Paul's letters, that membership in the church calls for certain responsibilities. These responsibilities are not a means of gaining salvation, but flow from the knowledge that God has chosen us and unites Himself with us and others within His church. We are called and chosen to support and uplift one another. Out of love for

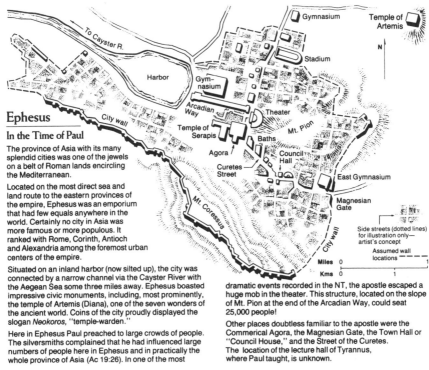

Ephesus

In the Time of Paul

The province of Asia with its many splendid cities was one of the jewels on a belt of Roman lands encircling the Mediterranean.

Located on the most direct sea and land route to the eastern provinces of the empire, Ephesus was an emporium that had few equals anywhere in the world. Certainly no city in Asia was more famous or more populous. It ranked with Rome, Corinth, Antioch and Alexandria among the foremost urban centers of the empire.

Situated on an inland harbor (now silted up), the city was connected by a narrow channel via the Cayster River with the Aegean Sea some three miles away. Ephesus boasted impressive civic monuments, including, most prominently, the temple of Artemis (Diana), one of the seven wonders of the ancient world. Coins of the city proudly displayed the slogan *Neokoros*, "temple-warden."

Here in Ephesus Paul preached to large crowds of people. The silversmiths complained that he had influenced large numbers of people here in Ephesus and in practically the whole province of Asia (Ac 19:26). In one of the most

dramatic events recorded in the NT, the apostle escaped a huge mob in the theater. This structure, located on the slope of Mt. Pion at the end of the Arcadian Way, could seat 25,000 people!

Other places doubtless familiar to the apostle were the Commerical Agora, the Magnesian Gate, the Town Hall or "Council House," and the Street of the Curetes. The location of the lecture hall of Tyrannus, where Paul taught, is unknown.

Jesus we constantly reach out to those who, while on the official roster, have separated themselves from the body of believers.

An Overview

Read Ephesians 2:1–10, 11–22, and Colossians 3:1–17. As you read, consider which sections describe how God creates His church and which parts describe what membership in the church involves.

The Message in Brief

As you read these portions from Paul's letters, you will notice that Ephesians 2 describes how the Lord brought us from sin and death into His saving arms. We were once exiled from God's kingdom without any hope of being redeemed. But because of Jesus' sacrificial death and glorious resurrection, we have been made citizens of that Kingdom, and indeed, members of the King's own family. This is how God continually establishes and expands His church.

The Colossians passage indicates that since we have been made God's people, we are called to demonstrate our love and faith in the Lord as our lives are transformed. We set our hearts and minds on that which is godly, attempting to "kill" the sinful nature. We know we will never be entirely successful in leading a God-pleasing life, but we rely upon the grace and forgiveness won by Jesus on the cross.

Working with the Text
How Does God Continually Build His Church?

1. After reading Ephesians 2:1–3, describe the lives of those who were "dead in … transgressions and sin." What were they by nature? How did they lead their lives? How does this section underscore the link between unbelief and sinful action?

2. Now read again Ephesians 2:4–10. How have the spiritually dead been raised? Who did it and why?

3. Describe how Paul defines the "process of salvation" in Ephesians 2:8–10. Who saves us? How are we *not* involved in this process? Are we able to brag about our "worthiness" in being saved? If not, to whom should we give total credit? How can we do this by our worship and praise?

4. Now read Ephesians 2:11–13. Describe the condition suffered by those who were formerly "separate from Christ." With what metaphor does Paul describe their alienation from God? Look at Eph-

esians 2:19 and indicate what blessing those who were once alienated now enjoy. How has the Lord gone beyond offering mere "citizenship" to those who follow Him?

5. What did Paul say in Galatians 3:26–29 about the unity and peace that followers of Christ enjoy? Now read Ephesians 2:14–18 and notice that when Jesus makes "the two one," He unites both Jew and Gentile under the lordship of Christ. How does this miracle of unity partially fulfill the angels' prophecy at Jesus' birth: "On earth peace to men on whom His favor rests" (Luke 2:14)?

> You are all sons of God through faith in Christ Jesus, for all of you who were baptized into Christ have clothed yourselves with Christ. There is neither Jew nor Greek, slave nor free, male nor female, for you are all one in Christ Jesus. If you belong to Christ, then you are Abraham's seed, and heirs according to the promise. Galatians 3:26–29

6. Reread Ephesians 2:19–22. What metaphor does Paul use to describe the church? On what foundation does the church rest, and who is its cornerstone? Extending the metaphor, who do you think makes up the building blocks of the church?

The Responsibilities of Membership

1. Read once again Ephesians 2:10. For what purpose did God save us? How does Paul's exhortation in Colossians 3:1–2 call us to this godly purpose?

2. To what specific attribute do followers of Christ aspire according to Colossians 3:14? Why do you think this is the most important quality of all?

3. What regular response does our faith call for according to Colossians 3:16 and Ephesians 5:19–20?

4. After reading Colossians 3:5–9, describe those traits which indicate a lack of "membership" in God's church.

5. Look up the following verses and further describe those responsibilities which flow from membership in the church:
   a. Ephesians 5:21–30; 6:1–8; Colossians 3:18–4:1

   b. Ephesians 4:28

   c. Ephesians 6:13–18

d. Colossians 2:8, 16–17

Applying the Message

1. Pastors are often concerned with those in the congregation who rarely attend worship and appear uninterested in supporting the work of the church. Such inactivity suggests something is missing in the member's faith life. If you were the pastor of a congregation, how would you deal with such a member?

2. Colossians declares that some laws are no longer in effect, while others remain important for Christian life. After reading Colossians 2:16–17 and Colossians 3:12–17, list those laws with which Christians need not be concerned. On the other hand, what laws remain important for Christian living?

3. Have you ever known anyone who has raised himself or herself from the dead? What does this suggest about Paul's description of people by nature being "dead in [their] transgressions and sins"? Can we by our own power raise ourselves from spiritual death? Explain again the "process of salvation" discussed in the last session.

4. In your opinion, what is the difference between being listed on the roster of a congregation and being a "member" of the church?

5. In Ephesians 2, Paul praises the Lord for breaking down the walls between Jew and Gentile. Colossians 3:11 confirms this miracle of unity. As the Holy Spirit works in the lives of members of the church, how do they come to view racial differences or differences in economic or social status? What does this suggest about the role of the church as an instrument of peace and unity in the local community?

Taking the Message Home

Review

After reading the texts again, consider the great love God showed by making us members of His church through Jesus Christ. Then consider how you can respond to His love by living a more God-pleasing life. Pray for the strength to amend those qualities which are not part of "membership," and ask the Lord for those characteristics that reflect that you are a child in His family.

Looking Ahead

In the next session we witness a divided and straying church located in the city of Corinth. Read 1 Corinthians 1:11–12. How could such division occur in your church? Consider what would happen if different "groups" within your congregation would refuse to work with one another. In what ways would the ministry of the church be affected? In what general manner would such a division have to be resolved?

Working Ahead

Choose one or more of the following for further study:

1. Ask a brother or sister in Christ if they have ever been familiar with a church suffering from division. Why was the congregation divided? What happened as a result of that division?

2. Read 1 Corinthians 5:1; 6:7; 11:20–22; 14:13–19; 15:12. List problems within the Corinthian congregation.

3. Read 2 Corinthians 11:21–29 and contemplate the tremendous suffering Paul endured during his ministry. Would you have the strength to persist through such difficulty? Why or why not?

Did you know that in the early church, Christians would worship in someone's home. The earliest example of a Christian house-church has been found in eastern Syria. The home was built about the year 232 and it was somewhat larger than an average house. One small room was used as a chapel. It had a small niche at one end with an arched roof above. Perhaps this was used as a baptismal font. A larger room was used for worship services and could hold about 100 people. At one end was a raised platform for the minister. Both rooms were covered in murals depicting Jesus' miracles.

Session 7

1–2 Corinthians:
the Church with Many Problems

1 Corinthians 3; 2 Corinthians 7:8–13

Approaching This Study

Some letters are difficult to write, especially when you have to tell your readers that they are disobeying the Lord's will. Surely the apostle Paul knew this. He loved people. He often praised his brothers and sisters in Christ and thanked the Lord for their presence. It was not easy

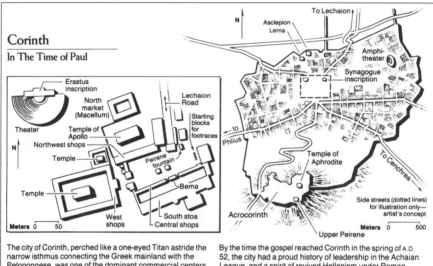

Corinth

In The Time of Paul

The city of Corinth, perched like a one-eyed Titan astride the narrow isthmus connecting the Greek mainland with the Peloponnese, was one of the dominant commercial centers of the Hellenic world as early as the eighth century B.C.

No city in Greece was more favorably situated for land and sea trade. With a high, strong citadel at its back, it lay between the Saronic Gulf and the Ionian Sea and ports at Lechaion and Cenchrea. A *diolkos*, or stone tramway for the overland transport of ships, linked the two seas. Crowning the Acrocorinth was the temple of Aphrodite, served, according to Strabo, by more than 1,000 pagan priestess-prostitutes.

By the time the gospel reached Corinth in the spring of A.D. 52, the city had a proud history of leadership in the Achaian League, and a spirit of revived Hellenism under Roman domination following the destruction of the city by Mummius in 146 B.C.

Paul's lengthy stay in Corinth brought him directly in contact with the major monuments of the *agora*, many of which still survive. The fountain-house of the spring *Peirene*, the temple of Apollo, the *macellum* or meat market (I Co 10:25), the theater, the *bema* (Ac 18:12), and the unimpressive synagogue all played a part in the experience of the apostle. An inscription from the theater names the city official Erastus, probably the friend of Paul mentioned in Ro 16:23.

for Paul to write a stern letter of correction. Especially when it applied to a congregation like Corinth. But because of Paul's devotion to the Lord and his love for people, he was compelled to write to the Christians in Corinth, trusting that as a result of his rebuke they would turn from their sin and receive the forgiveness Jesus had won for them on the cross.

The Corinthian Christians lived in a rich, cosmopolitan city that had little use for God. The citizens were more interested in their pagan gods, particularly the goddess of love, Aphrodite. As a matter of fact, they worshiped the goddess through the use of temple prostitutes. So Corinth was a particularly immoral, wealthy city. It's no wonder that the Corinthian Christians were beset by so many conflicts and quarrels. They were being tempted by many sinful influences.

Could we compare much of American society with the culture of Corinth? Evidence suggests that Americans rely less and less on the Lord. Just like the Corinthian Christians, Americans have never really known persecution for the faith. American television, movies, and literature tempt us with the same sort of immoral activities that surrounded the Christians in Corinth. These influences encourage quarrels and divisions in our churches just as they did in Paul's day.

When Paul heard about the Corinthians' problems, quarrels, and errors, he wrote them a letter. The members of the congregation became alarmed by his words and, as a result, took action to correct their ways. When Paul wrote them a second time, he was able to praise them for their growth resulting from the forgiveness God had provided them through faith in Christ Jesus.

An Overview

Read 1 Corinthians 3 and 2 Corinthians 7:8–13 and notice how Paul's first letter criticizes the Corinthians for their jealousies and quarrels whereas the second letter praises them for repenting and demonstrating the love and forgiveness Jesus won for them on the cross.

The Message in Brief

The Corinthian church was racked by division. There were separate and opposing groups within the congregation, all claiming superiority over the others. As a result of their quarreling, many errant beliefs and practices infiltrated the congregation. Paul condemned the Corinthians for their misguided ways, hoping to shock them into repentance. When the Corinthians did repent, Paul expressed his joy and love for them, praising God for their reversal.

Working with the Texts

The Corinthians' Many Problems (1 Corinthians 3)

1. What does 1 Corinthians 3:1–4 tell us about the cause of the quarreling within the Corinthian church? How is this supported by 1 Corinthians 1:11–12?

2. What was Apollos' background? How would you describe him after reading this brief account found in Acts 18:24–28? What kind of intellect did he possess? How would you describe his talent as a preacher and evangelist?

> Meanwhile a Jew named Apollos, a native of Alexandria, came to Ephesus. He was a learned man, with a thorough knowledge of the Scriptures. He had been instructed in the way of the Lord, and he spoke with great fervor and taught about Jesus accurately, though he knew only the baptism of John. He began to speak boldly in the synagogue. When Priscilla and Aquila heard him, they invited him to their home and explained to him the way of God more adequately.
>
> When Apollos wanted to go to Achaia, the brothers encouraged him and wrote to the disciples there to welcome him. On arriving, he was a great help to those who by grace had believed. For he vigorously refuted the Jews in public debate, proving from the Scriptures that Jesus was the Christ. Acts 18:24–28

3. Now look at the description of Paul in 1 Corinthians 2:1–4 and 2 Corinthians 10:7–11. In contrast to Apollos, how would you evaluate Paul's talents at preaching? After Paul left Corinth, Apollos became their

pastor. Can you think of reasons why some would view Paul as a superior spiritual leader to Apollos and vice versa?

4. What does Paul have to say about other major congregational problems and their solutions?

a. 1 Corinthians 5:1–5

b. 1 Corinthians 6:1–8

c. 1 Corinthians 6:13–20

d. 1 Corinthians 11:17–34

e. 1 Corinthians 15:12–24

The Corinthians Repent (2 Corinthians 7:8–13)

1. How did Paul feel when he wrote his first letter to the Corinthians according to 2 Corinthians 2:4? What was the result of that letter (2 Corinthians 7:8–9)?

2. Clearly, Paul felt as if he needed to stress his qualifications as an apostle to the Corinthians. Some in Corinth were claiming to follow more "authentic" apostles such as Peter and were attempting to diminish Paul's importance. Read 2 Corinthians 11:16–12:13 and list the ways in which Paul suffered for the faith, thereby supporting his authority for spiritual leadership.

3. Now look at 2 Corinthians 4:16–18 and explain why Paul could endure all these troubles.

4. In his first letter, Paul exhorts the Corinthians to help raise an offering for the Christians in Jerusalem. Read 1 Corinthians 16:1–5. How were the Corinthians to collect this offering? Who will Paul visit before coming to Corinth for the offering? Now look up 2 Corinthians 8:1–9. What was the result of the collection from Macedonia as Paul made his way to Corinth? What does a generous offering suggest about the faith of the givers?

5. Because of the Christian's faith and love for the Lord, what kind of attitude should be expressed in the giving of offerings according to 2 Corinthians 9:6–8?

Applying the Message

1. Do you think it's good for people to compare the good and bad points of different pastors or other leaders? Why or why not? Look up 1 Corinthians 3:5–7, 21–23, and explain how these verses answer the question.

2. Consider your own congregation. Do the members sometimes argue about issues which aren't really important? If so, why do such things happen? What do you think could be done about such quarreling? Could you help resolve the differences? How?

3. Turn to 1 Corinthians 12:12–27 and explain what perspective these words bring to quarrels within the congregation. What happens to the mission of the congregation when one group quarrels with another?

4. Paul stressed the need for love to motivate and inspire our Christian witness. His most profound exposition on love is found in 1 Corinthians 13. Read it and discuss the qualities of Christian love.

How does it differ from "love" as presented on television and in the movies? Would you say Christian love is a matter of feelings or commitment? Why? How can we view God's love in a similar manner?

5. What does Paul have to say about separating ourselves from unbelievers in 2 Corinthians 6:14–18? How might you apply this to the selection of a husband or wife in marriage?

6. After reading 1 Corinthians 7:1–2, 8–9, how would you describe Paul's attitude toward marriage? Is his attitude sufficient reason to demand that spiritual leaders abstain from marriage? Before answering, consider 1 Corinthians 9:3–6.

7. Read about Paul's problem in 2 Corinthians 12:7–10. No one knows precisely with what affliction Paul was burdened. But what does his response suggest about the reason for suffering?

Taking the Message Home

Review

Read again the Scripture references from this session. Spend a few minutes in prayer, asking that the Lord would bless your congregation with peace and unity so that by your words and actions others might come to confess Jesus as Lord and Savior.

Looking Ahead

Read Matthew 24 and list the signs that will usher in the end of the ages. Which of these signs do you see fulfilled today? Are there any which are not yet fulfilled?

Working Ahead

Choose one or more of the following for further study:

1. Spend a few minutes contemplating what you would do if the world were to end tomorrow. Would you reconcile with your enemies? Would you give all your money to the poor? Write down the possibilities and be ready to share them at the next session.

2. Do you remember a movie that depicted the end of the world? What brought about the earth's demise? Was there any hope for deliverance in the end?

3. Look up 1 Thessalonians 4:13–18 and express in your own words how you picture the coming of Jesus Christ on the Last Day. Try to be as imaginative as possible without going beyond that which Scripture teaches.

Did you know that in Romans 16:23 Paul sends greetings to the Roman church from a man named "Erastus, who is the city's director of public works." Paul is writing his letter from Corinth. At Corinth archaeologists have discovered a block of stone in a paved square with the Latin inscription: "Erastus, commissioner of public works, bore the expense of this pavement!"

St. Paul Preaching to the Thessalonians by Gustave Doré

For ye remember, brethren, our labour and travail: for labouring night and day ... we preached unto you the gospel of God (1 Thessalonians 2:9 KJV). From *The Doré Bible Illustrated*. By permission of Dover Publications, Inc.

Session 8

Philippians; 1–2 Thessalonians: When the End Seems Near

Philippians 3:12–21; 1 Thessalonians 4:13–5:3; 2 Thessalonians 2:1–12

Approaching This Study

Everyone knows the world will not last forever. Scientists tell us that in several eons, the sun will burn out. As it dies it will expand and incinerate the earth. Christians also know that the world will not last forever, but there is more immediacy to our understanding about the end of the world. For one thing, Jesus spoke about it with a sense of urgency, warning us to be ready for His return at any moment. "No one knows about that day or hour," Jesus said, "not even the angels in heaven, nor the Son, but only the Father" (Matthew 24:36). For another thing, even as God created the universe instantly with His Word, so we know He has the power to end it at any moment. Christians aren't persuaded by those who claim the end of the world may happen eons in the future. We believe Jesus could come today or tomorrow.

Spend a few minutes and share with each other what you would do if you knew the end of the world would arrive tomorrow.

Even as many scientists predict the earth will remain intact for untold millennia, so there were those in Paul's day who claimed that since Jesus had not yet returned, He would probably not come at all. Other members of the church were confused about the meaning of Christ's return, thinking that if the end was imminent, they could quit work! These opposing viewpoints instigated Paul's two letters to the Thessalonians, instructing them about the end of the world. He reminded them that Christ's return would be sudden and unexpected, and those who were unprepared would face condemnation. He also told the Thessalonians that while they waited for the Lord's return, they should work. They were not to engage in idleness.

In Philippians, often known as "the letter of joy," Paul praises the Christians for their faithfulness and support and encourages them to keep pursuing the Christian life. Their real home is in heaven, and they

Philippi In the Time of Paul

The Roman colony of Philippi (*Colonia Augusta Julia Philippensis*) was an important city in Macedonia, located on the main highway leading from the eastern provinces to Rome. This road, the Via Egnatia, bisected the city's forum and was the chief cause of its prosperity and political importance. Ten miles distant on the coast was Neapolis, the place where Paul landed after sailing from Troas, in response to the Macedonian vision.

As a prominent city of the gold-producing region of Macedonia, Philippi had a proud history. Named originally after Philip II, the father of Alexander the Great, the city was later honored with the name of Julius Caesar and Augustus. Many Italian settlers from the legions swelled the ranks of citizens and made Philippi vigorous and polyglot. It grew from a small settlement to a city of dignity and privilege. Among its highest honors was the *ius Italicum*, by which it enjoyed rights legally equivalent to those of Italian cities.

Ruins of the theater, the acropolis, the forum, the baths, and the western commemorative arch mentioned as the "gate" of the city in Ac 16:13 have been found. A little farther beyond the arch at the Gangites River is the place where Paul addressed some God-fearing women and where Lydia was converted.

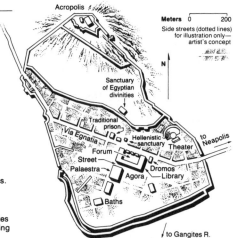

Taken from NIV STUDY BIBLE. Copyright © 1985 by the Zondervan Corporation. Used by permission of Zondervan Publishing House.

are to await with steadfastness and patience the day when Christ would change them from their "lowly bodies so that they will be like His glorious body."

An Overview

Read Philippians 3:12–21; 1 Thessalonians 4:13–5:3; and 2 Thessalonians 2:1–12. Which is your favorite selection and why?

The Message in Brief

In the first letter to the Thessalonians Paul hopes to comfort the Christians by explaining that those who have already died in the Lord will accompany the living into salvation. We need not worry when a loved one in the Lord dies before we do. We will see that person again when Christ comes with the sound of the archangel and his trumpet. Because of some people's reaction to his letter—and a subsequent rumor which followed—Paul sent a second letter to Thessalonica explaining that the Lord's return could not be expected until the "man of lawlessness" was revealed. In Philippians, Paul exhorts us to remain diligent in Christian living as we await the coming of the Lord. We are to "press on" toward the moment when we are given our eternal reward through Jesus Christ.

Working with the Text

Philippians 3:13–21: Press On in Joy!

1. As Paul anticipates eternal life with his Lord, he forgets "what is behind and strain[s] toward what is ahead" (3:13). What a tremendous lesson for us! Wouldn't life be much more peaceful and rich if we could leave behind our sinful pasts and look forward to the love and guidance of God's Spirit? Look up Philippians 1:18; 3:1; and 4:4–7. To what emotion does Paul's understanding of Christ's love lead him? How would this emotion help Paul remain undisturbed by the people who tried to make life hard for him (1:15–18)?

2. How does the Christian life differ from other lifestyles according to Philippians 3:19–21? What does it mean to you that our "lowly bodies" will be transformed into those which are like "His glorious body"? Does 1 Corinthians 15:42–49 help explain your answer? How?

> So will it be with the resurrection of the dead. The body that is sown is perishable, it is raised imperishable; it is sown in dishonor, it is raised in glory; it is sown in weakness, it is raised in power; it is sown a natural body, it is raised a spiritual body.
>
> If there is a natural body, there is also a spiritual body. So it is written: "The first man Adam became a living being"; the last Adam, a life-giving spirit. The spiritual did not come first, but the natural, and after that the spiritual. The first man was of the dust of the earth, the second man from heaven. As was the earthly man, so are those who are of the earth; and as is the man from heaven, so also are those who are of heaven. And just as we have borne the likeness of the earthly man, so shall we bear the likeness of the man from heaven. 1 Corinthians 15:42–49

1 Thessalonians 4:13–18: The Coming of the Lord!

1. The description of the resurrection is not something concocted by Paul's imagination. It is not simply his opinion. It has been provided "according to the Lord's own word." So we can trust it. What does verse 15 tell you about the human condition upon the Lord's arrival? Will people still exist or will they have become extinct? According to Matthew 16:18 will God's church still exist as well?

> And I tell you that you are Peter, and on this rock I will build My church, and the gates of Hades will not overcome it. Matthew 16:18

2. Compare 1 Thessalonians 4:16 with other descriptions of Judgment Day, particularly Matthew 13:41; 24:31; 25:31; Revelation 11:15, and Acts 1:10–11. What do they have in common?

> The Son of Man will send out His angels, and they will weed out of His kingdom everything that causes sin and all who do evil. Matthew 13:41

> And He will send His angels with a loud trumpet call, and they will gather His elect from the four winds, from one end of the heavens to the other. Matthew 24:31

> "When the Son of Man comes in His glory, and all the angels with Him, He will sit on His throne in heavenly glory. Matthew 25:31

> The seventh angel sounded his trumpet, and there were loud voices in heaven, which said: "The kingdom of the world has become the kingdom of our Lord and of His Christ, and He will reign for ever and ever." Revelation 11:15

> They were looking intently up into the sky as He was going, when suddenly two men dressed in white stood beside them. "Men of Galilee," they said, "why do you stand here looking into the sky? This same Jesus, who has been taken from you into heaven, will come back in the same way you have seen Him go into heaven." Acts 1:10–11

3. What happens to both the living and the dead when the Lord returns according to 1 Thessalonians 4:17? Will this apply only to believers? (Check Matthew 25:31–46.)

"When the Son of Man comes in His glory, and all the angels with Him, He will sit on His throne in heavenly glory. All the nations will be gathered before Him, and He will separate the people one from another as a shepherd separates the sheep from the goats. He will put the sheep on His right and the goats on His left.

Then the King will say to those on His right, 'Come, you who are blessed by My Father; take your inheritance, the kingdom prepared for you since the creation of the world. For I was hungry and you gave Me something to eat, I was thirsty and you gave Me something to drink, I was a stranger and you invited Me in, I needed clothes and you clothed Me, I was sick and you looked after Me, I was in prison and you came to visit Me.'

"Then the righteous will answer Him, 'Lord, when did we see You hungry and feed You, or thirsty and give You something to drink? When did we see You a stranger and invite You in, or needing clothes and clothe You? When did we see You sick or in prison and go to visit You?'

"The King will reply, 'I tell you the truth, whatever you did for one of the least of these brothers of Mine, you did for Me.'

"Then He will say to those on His left, 'Depart from Me, you who are cursed, into the eternal fire prepared for the devil and his angels. For I was hungry and you gave Me nothing to eat, I was thirsty and you gave Me nothing to drink, I was a stranger and you did not invite Me in, I needed clothes and you did not clothe Me, I was sick and in prison and you did not look after Me.'

"They also will answer, 'Lord, when did we see You hungry or thirsty or a stranger or needing clothes or sick or in prison, and did not help You?'

"He will reply, 'I tell you the truth, whatever you did not do for one of the least of these, you did not do for Me.'

"Then they will go away to eternal punishment, but the righteous to eternal life." Matthew 25:31–46

4. Look at 1 Thessalonians 5:1–3; Luke 12:40; and 2 Peter 3:10. How quickly and unexpectedly will Christ's arrival be? What does this suggest about the way we should live our lives each day?

> "You also must be ready, because the Son of Man will come at an hour when you do not expect Him." Luke 12:40

> But the day of the Lord will come like a thief. The heavens will disappear with a roar; the elements will be destroyed by fire, and the earth and everything in it will be laid bare. 2 Peter 3:10

2 Thessalonians 2:1–12: The Man of Lawlessness

1. The reaction to Paul's first letter was disturbing. Look up 2 Thessalonians 2:2 and 3:6–12. Try to explain how the imminence of the Lord's return may have affected some Christians in Thessalonica.

2. To settle down the excited Thessalonians, Paul explained that Jesus would not come until the arrival of the "man of lawlessness." In the following verses, what do we learn about this "man"?

a. 2 Thessalonians 2:4

b. 2 Thessalonians 2:7

c. 2 Thessalonians 2:9–12

3. To whom might this "man of lawlessness" apply? Can you think of any historical figures who might fit? Do you think we can be certain about any of them? What does this suggest about our preparation for the Lord's coming?

4. As we await the second coming of Jesus Christ, how do we live our lives according to 2 Thessalonians 2:13–17 and 1 Thessalonians 5:4–22? Have you noticed how often Paul stresses the kind of lifestyle which naturally flows from faith in the Lord?

Applying the Message

1. How would you describe a life of joy in the Lord? Does it mean simply walking around with a smile on one's face all day? How do you think Christian joy affects our relationships, our daily chores, and our general attitude?

2. How would you describe Paul's "tact" according to 1 Thessalonians 2:2–6? Is this a good quality or bad quality in a pastor? How did the Thessalonians accept it according to 2:13?

3. Do you think happiness could be based on the material things of this world? Would it be possible, for example, to be happy at Christmas if one received no presents? Consider Paul's remarks in Philippians 4:11–13. How was he able to find joy and contentment without material goods? Could we learn to do this, too? In what way?

4. Consider 1 Thessalonians 1:2–10. Why do Christians enjoy fellowship with each other? Do Paul's words suggest an important reason for regular worship and Bible study with brothers and sisters in Christ? What is that reason?

5. Why are Christians expected to stay busy? Read 1 Thessalonians 4:11–13 and 2 Thessalonians 3:6–13. Suggest some reasons why busy Christians can lead a more exemplary life than those who are idle. Share with others those things you could do in order to remain "busy."

6. When Paul writes to the Philippians, he suggests they set their hearts and minds on uplifting thoughts, ideas, and goals. As you read Philippians 4:8–9, what do Paul's words suggest about the kind of art and literature we should enjoy? Does it have anything to say about which thoughts and ideas are best for us to embrace?

7. One last intriguing note. Under what circumstance is Paul writing this letter according to Philippians 1:7–17? Now consider Philippians 4:21–22. From what city does Paul appear to be writing? And who is

sharing the faith with him? What does this suggest about the influence of Paul's faith?

Taking the Message Home

Review

Read again the Scripture references from this session. List the blessings for which you are particularly thankful and explain how each gives you joy in the Lord. Then contemplate how your present joys will be surpassed by those anticipated in heaven. Make another list of the people you look forward to seeing in heaven.

Looking Ahead

Read Acts 16:1–5 and notice Timothy's background. Then read Philippians 2:19–23 to discover Timothy's importance to Paul. Finally, read Galatians 2:1–5 to gather some background on Titus. Be prepared to share what you have learned about these two pastors during the next session.

Working Ahead

Choose one or more of the following for further study:

1. List those qualifications you feel are most important in a pastor. Be open to revising your opinion after the next session!

2. Consider the importance of a pastor being grounded in correct doctrine. What would happen if a pastor were unsure of his beliefs? How would his uncertainties affect the spiritual health of the congregation?

3. Before the next session, spend some time considering the role of the church in politics. Is it appropriate for Christians to "take up arms" against a government which demands its citizens to act ungodly? How should Christians work to change the "status quo" when a government is disobeying God's Law? Be prepared to discuss these questions during the next session.

Did you know that the catacombs in Rome and other cities were built during the early centuries of Christianity? They were composed of extensive underground tunnels and chambers where the dead were buried in compartments along the walls. Christians would gather there during periods of persecution for secret worship services. They would also hold communal meals there. The catacombs were decorated with frescoes of biblical scenes. A common picture was that of the fish. The Greek word for fish, *ixthus*, was formed from the first letters of the Greek words meaning, "Jesus Christ, Son of God, Savior."

According to tradition, both Peter and Paul were held captive in Rome's Mamertine Prison (above) during Nero's persecution of the Christians. The lightless interior cell of this prison was 12 feet underground, and as originally designed it could be reached only through a hole in the ceiling. Photo by permission of Eric Lessing/Art Resource.

Session 9

1–2 Timothy; Titus; Philemon: Letters to Two Pastors and a Slave Owner

1 Timothy 3:1–7; 4:1–16; 2 Timothy 4:1–8; Titus 3:1–11; Philemon

Approaching This Study

Almost all congregations have pastors. Someone must lead a congregation in its spiritual growth and outreach. Whoever fills that role will find comfort in affirmation and will seek new ways to strengthen the congregation's ministry.

So we shouldn't be surprised that the New Testament incorporates three letters that focus on the pastoral work of the church. They are often called, appropriately, "the pastoral letters" to Timothy and Titus. It is likely that Titus, a Gentile, was older than Timothy because Paul selected Titus for some special assignments. Furthermore, Paul refers to Timothy's youth, encouraging him not to be intimidated by those who might consider him immature. When Paul wrote his second letter to Timothy, he was in prison. Most of his friends had deserted him, and he felt lonely. But he continued to look forward to the heavenly home God had prepared for him.

In Philemon, Paul is concerned about a slave named Onesimus who had fled from his owner. We are not told why Onesimus ran away, but somehow he became a follower of Christ and a special helper to the apostle Paul. In fact, Paul would have preferred to keep Onesimus as his helper, but instead, wrote Philemon and asked him to accept the returning Onesimus and to treat him as a fellow Christian.

Paul's exhortations in the pastoral letters and Philemon demonstrate how followers of Christ find themselves transformed. Those who know and love the Lord find their selfish natures diminished. By the working of the Holy Spirit the Christian begins to think of others, reflecting the wondrous love God has given us in Jesus Christ.

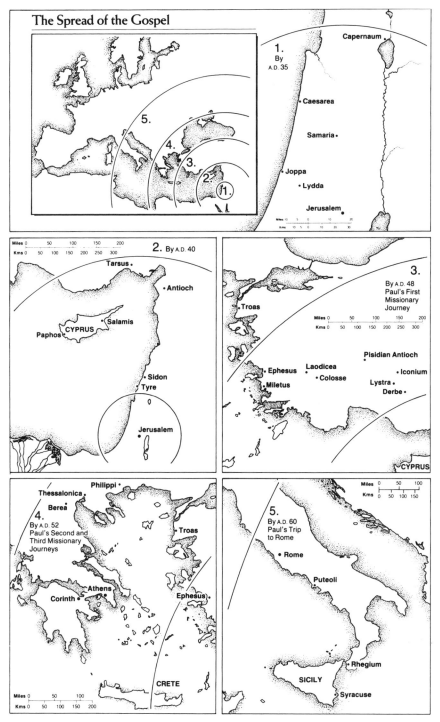

The Spread of the Gospel

1. By A.D. 35

Capernaum

Caesarea

Samaria

Joppa

Lydda

Jerusalem

Miles 10 5 0   10   20
Kms 10 5 0   10   20   30

2. By A.D. 40

Miles 0   50   100   150   200
Kms 0   50   100   150   200   250   300

Tarsus

Antioch

CYPRUS   Salamis

Paphos

Sidon
Tyre

Jerusalem

3. By A.D. 48 Paul's First Missionary Journey

Troas

Miles 0   50   100   150   200
Kms 0   50   100   150   200   250   300

Pisidian Antioch

Ephesus   Laodicea
Colosse   Iconium

Miletus   Lystra
Derbe

CYPRUS

4. By A.D. 52 Paul's Second and Third Missionary Journeys

Philippi

Thessalonica

Berea

Troas

Athens

Corinth

Ephesus

CRETE

Miles 0   50   100
Kms 0   50   100   150   200

5. By A.D. 60 Paul's Trip to Rome

Miles 0   50   100
Kms 0   50   100   150

Rome

Puteoli

Rhegium

SICILY

Syracuse

An Overview

Read aloud 1 Timothy 3:1–7; 4:1–16; 2 Timothy 4:1–8; Titus 3:1–11; and Philemon.

The Message in Brief

After Paul had left Timothy at Ephesus to preach the Word, Paul reminds the young pastor about the core of God's Gospel message. Paul emphasizes that there is one Mediator between God and man, Jesus Christ. Jesus came to earth for the purpose of saving sinners. Paul's second letter to Timothy is, in effect, Paul's last will and testament. Paul knows his end is near, and he encourages Timothy to continue proclaiming the message of God's grace. Paul's letter to Titus also emphasizes God's grace in Jesus Christ which is given to us through the working of the Holy Spirit in Baptism. Finally, in Philemon, Paul intercedes on behalf of a runaway slave named Onesimus, encouraging his owner to receive Onesimus as a fellow brother in Christ. All four letters emphasize the transforming power of God's grace as it touches people's minds and hearts.

Working with the Text

1 Timothy 3:1–7; 4:1–16: a Letter of Support to a Young Pastor

1. It would be natural for an experienced apostle like Paul to explain the qualifications of "pastor" to a young man such as Timothy. After reading 1 Timothy 3:1–7, list in your own words the pastor's necessary qualifications. What does Paul suggest about the pastor's gender? Why do you think it is important that someone seeking the office of the ministry should not be a recent convert?

2. In 1 Timothy 4:1–4 Paul warns Timothy about the religious deceptions a pastor and his laypeople will confront. These deceptive teachings will inevitably lead some astray from the true faith. When such false teachers are described, they appear to "forbid people to marry and

order them to abstain from certain foods." In Paul's day, this probably referred to an ascetic branch of Gnostic heretics. Look up *Gnostic* (or *Gnosticism*) in a Bible dictionary and describe this false teaching. Does Paul's warning remind you of some false teachings we may hear today? What are they?

3. Read again verses 12–16. What do Paul's words suggest about Timothy's age? How is Timothy to overcome this "disadvantage"? And what are to be Timothy's primary tasks as a pastor?

2 Timothy 4:1–8: Paul's Last Letter

1. Again, what is Timothy's primary task as a pastor according to verses 2–5? Why is this such an important role for the shepherd of a congregation? Do you think there are those today who would prefer to have their "itching ears" scratched? Describe contemporary examples.

2. What do you think verses 6–8 suggest about Paul's future? With what mixed feelings does Paul anticipate his end? Before you answer, also read 2 Timothy 1:15 and 4:18.

3. Read 2 Timothy 3:1–5 and compare Paul's description of people living in the last days with people living today. Is there really anything "new under the sun?" Why or why not?

Titus 3: 1–11: a Letter to a Pastor in Crete

1. According to Titus 1:5, what is to be Pastor Titus's responsibility? Where was his geographical area of work?

2. What does Paul say is the Christian's responsibility toward government according to Titus 3:1? How is that confirmed by Jesus in Matthew 22:15–21 and by 1 Peter 2:13–14 and Romans 13:1–7? Isn't it rather remarkable that such words of submission toward government should to be repeated to Christians who were already facing persecution under the Roman rule? According to Acts 5:25–29, however, when should a Christian refuse to submit to government?

> Then the Pharisees went out and laid plans to trap Him in His words. They sent their disciples to Him along with the Herodians. "Teacher," they said, "we know You are a man of integrity and that You teach the way of God in accordance with the truth. You aren't swayed by men, because You pay no attention to who they are. Tell us then, what is Your opinion? Is it right to pay taxes to Caesar or not?"
>
> But Jesus, knowing their evil intent, said, "You hypocrites, why are you trying to trap Me? Show Me the coin used for paying the tax." They brought Him a denarius, and He asked them, "Whose portrait is this? And whose inscription?"
>
> "Caesar's," they replied. Then He said to them, "Give to Caesar what is Caesar's, and to God what is God's." Matthew 22:15–21

> Submit yourselves for the Lord's sake to every authority instituted among men: whether to the king, as the supreme authority, or to governors, who are sent by him to punish those who do wrong and to commend those who do right. 1 Peter 2:13–14

> Everyone must submit himself to the governing authorities, for there is no authority except that which God has established. The authorities that exist have been established by God. Consequently, he who rebels against the authority is rebelling against what God has instituted, and those who do so will bring judgment on themselves. For rulers hold no terror for those who do right, but for those who do wrong. Do you want to be free from fear of the one in authority? Then do what is right and he will commend you. For he is God's servant to do you good. But if you do

wrong, be afraid, for he does not bear the sword for nothing. He is God's servant, an agent of wrath to bring punishment on the wrongdoer. Therefore, it is necessary to submit to the authorities, not only because of possible punishment but also because of conscience.

This is also why you pay taxes, for the authorities are God's servants, who give their full time to governing. Give everyone what you owe him: If you owe taxes, pay taxes; if revenue, then revenue; if respect, then respect; if honor, then honor. Romans 13:1–7

Then someone came and said, "Look! The men you put in jail are standing in the temple courts teaching the people." At that, the captain went with his officers and brought the apostles. They did not use force, because they feared that the people would stone them.

Having brought the apostles, they made them appear before the Sanhedrin to be questioned by the high priest. "We gave you strict orders not to teach in this name," he said. "Yet you have filled Jerusalem with your teaching and are determined to make us guilty of this man's blood."

Peter and the other apostles replied: "We must obey God rather than men!" Acts 5:25–29

3. Read again Titus 3:3–8. What kind of transformation does the Gospel of Jesus Christ bring to those who receive it? The Bible claims that God brings salvation through certain "means." What is one "means" He uses according to Titus 3:5?

4. What should be the church member's attitude toward those who are argumentative and divisive? What does this suggest about those who would tolerate any kind of behavior in the church for fear of causing "offense"? How can a congregation be more proactive in fending off unnecessary conflict and division within its ranks?

Philemon: a Letter to a Slave Owner

1. How does Paul feel about his friend Philemon according to verses 4–7? Why?

2. After reading verses 8–16, explain Onesimus' history. When did Paul meet him? What is Paul's feeling toward Onesimus? What does Paul encourage Onesimus to do? And what should Philemon's attitude be toward his former slave?

3. Paul's request of Philemon is a great one. He is to accept voluntarily Onesimus and begin to treat him like a brother in Christ. How will Paul learn about whether Philemon follows through on Paul's request (verse 22)?

4. Read the following passages and express your understanding of how Paul viewed slavery: Ephesians 6:5–8; Colossians 3:22–25; 1 Timothy 6:1–2; Titus 2:9–10. Did he advocate the overthrow of this evil and abusive system? How were Christian masters to treat their slaves?

> Slaves, obey your earthly masters with respect and fear, and with sincerity of heart, just as you would obey Christ. Obey them not only to win their favor when their eye is on you, but like slaves of Christ, doing the will of God from your heart. Serve wholeheartedly, as if you were serving the Lord, not men, because you know that the Lord will reward everyone for whatever good he does, whether he is slave or free. Ephesians 6:5–8

> Slaves, obey your earthly masters in everything; and do it, not only when their eye is on you and to win their favor, but with sincerity of heart and reverence for the Lord. Whatever you do, work at it with all your heart, as working for the Lord, not for men, since you know that you will receive an inheritance from the Lord as a reward. It is the Lord Christ you are serving. Anyone who does wrong will be repaid for his wrong, and there is no favoritism. Colossians 3:22–25

All who are under the yoke of slavery should consider their masters worthy of full respect, so that God's name may not be slandered. Those who have believing masters are not to show less respect for them because they are brothers. Instead, they are to serve them even better, because those who benefit from their service are believers, and dear to them. These are the things you are to teach and urge on them. 1 Timothy 6:1–2

Teach slaves to be subject to their masters in everything, to try to please them, not to talk back to them, and not to steal from them, but to show that they can be fully trusted, so that in every way they will make the teaching about God our Savior attractive. Titus 2:9–10

5. Read Ephesians 6:7–9 and Colossians 4:1. How does the letter to Philemon demonstrate Paul's method of changing "the system" in a God-pleasing manner?

Serve wholeheartedly, as if you were serving the Lord, not men, because you know that the Lord will reward everyone for whatever good he does, whether he is slave or free.

And masters, treat your slaves in the same way. Do not threaten them, since you know that He who is both their Master and yours is in heaven, and there is no favoritism with Him. Ephesians 6:7–9

Masters, provide your slaves with what is right and fair, because you know that you also have a Master in heaven. Colossians 4:1

Applying the Message

1. After thinking about the qualifications for a pastor, consider those abilities which are NOT mentioned. Do you think a pastor is called to to be a good administrator, or financial officer, or an organizational genius?

Must he be the smartest person in the congregation? Explain in your own words the one quality you think is most important for the pastor.

2. Read again 2 Timothy 3:1–5 and consider modern examples of these disturbing behaviors. In what ways do you think our world has become rude, greedy, and decadent? Cite some examples. In what way can a Christian witness his or her faith simply by remaining polite?

3. The relationship of a Christian toward his government can sometimes be confusing depending on whether a Christian believes his or her faith is being compromised by the government's demands. Consider the following examples and express your view of the church's involvement in

a. bombing abortion clinics;

b. peacefully demonstrating against a proposal to legalize euthanasia.

Taking the Message Home

Review

Review the Scripture references for this session. These are the last letters from Paul we will read. Having read a number of Paul's writings, how would you describe his personality? Is he a tactful person? Does he write simple sentences with easily understood thoughts? Does he demonstrate love and concern for his readers? Share your opinions with each other.

Looking Ahead

Next session we will consider three more letters. The author of Hebrews is unknown, but James and Jude appear to be letters written by Jesus' brothers. For the next session be sure to read various selections from these letters, including James 2, Jude, and Hebrews 7.

Working Ahead

Choose one or more of the following for further study:

1. Consider Mark 6:1–6. Early in His ministry, Jesus returned to Nazareth so that He could teach in the synagogue. Naturally, there were people present who remembered Jesus' childhood and family. According to Jesus' acquaintances, what were the names of His brothers? What does it mean to you that Jesus was only one sibling among a larger family?

2. Before the next session, discover the function of the Old Testament priest by reading Leviticus 4:13–21; Exodus 20:18–21; and Leviticus 16:1–7. Be prepared to describe how God would work through the priest to offer forgiveness to His people. Then contemplate what the author of Hebrews means when he calls Jesus "our great high priest."

3. Consider the purpose of model airplanes, cars, and ships. Why do children enjoy them so much? What do they imagine when they play with such toys? How are these toys representations of that which is real? Then read Colossians 2:16–17 and think about the symbols we use to represent important events. For example, we use fireworks on the Fourth of July to remind us of the battles our country endured to secure independence. We hide Easter eggs to remind us of our new birth in Jesus Christ. We give each other presents at Christmas as a reminder of God's gift in Jesus Christ. According to Colossians, what was the function of many Old Testament political and ceremonial laws?

Did you know that the word *bishop* means "overseer"? Over the passing of time, a hierarchy of pastors emerged in the early Christian Church. Individuals who were heads of city or town congregations began overseeing the pastors of congregations in the surrounding area. In time there evolved bishops of bishops, giving rise to archbishops and the Pope.

Session 10

Hebrews; James; Jude: Letters That Define "Faith"

Hebrews 7; James 2; Jude

Approaching This Study

Some people are fascinated by putting together model airplanes, boats, cars, or ships. They spend hours constructing detailed replicas. One of Hebrews' purposes is to illustrate how some Old Testament stories and ceremonial laws were "models" for God's plan of salvation through Jesus Christ. In this session we will particularly reflect on a mysterious Old Testament figure named Melchizedek, who acted as a "model" or "type" of Jesus Christ. Such Old Testament "modeling" prepared us for the ministry of Jesus Christ and demonstrates why the history of Israel remains important for Christians.

The letter of James stresses the deeds which naturally flow from genuine faith. It is relatively easy to speak faithful words. It is more difficult to demonstrate faith by our deeds. Faith which is genuine should not just "talk the talk, " but also "walk the walk." James emphasizes that our faith must lead to godly deeds and actions.

The letter from Jude illustrates the need to defend our faith against false teachers. The church will always confront those who wish to alter God's pure Word; the Christian must discern that which is false and avoid it.

An Overview

Hebrews 7 is rather complex. As it is read, focus on the function of Melchizedek, but don't be too concerned about understanding every point. James 2 is much more understandable, connecting Christian faith to charitable deeds. Jude's warning against false doctrine and immoral behavior is equally clear.

The Message in Brief

In Genesis 14:18–20 we encounter a meeting between the great patriarch, Abraham, and the king of Salem known as Melchizedek. The author of Hebrews models the ministry of Jesus Christ around this mysterious king, and thereby illustrates Jesus' function as our great high priest. James points out that our faith in Jesus as God's great sacrifice for sin serves to inspire us to perform charitable and loving deeds. Jude stresses that the preservation of our faith requires that we discern truth from error.

Working with the Text

Hebrews 7: Jesus As Priest and King

1. First read Hebrews 7:1–10. Then read Genesis 14:18–20. Compare the story of Melchizedek in Genesis with the Hebrews interpretation. Then answer the following questions with the understanding that Melchizedek is a "model" of Jesus Christ.

> Then Melchizedek king of Salem brought out bread and wine. He was priest of God Most High, and he blessed Abram, saying,
> > "Blessed be Abram by God Most High,
> > > Creator of heaven and earth.
> > And blessed be God Most High,
> > > who delivered your enemies into your hand."
> Then Abram gave him a tenth of everything. Genesis 14:18–20

a. What does the name "Melchizedek" mean according to Hebrews? Identify the kingdom over which Melchizedek ruled. What does Hebrews say "Salem" means? What other function did Melchizedek fulfill other than "king"? How do all of these descriptive details depict Melchizedek as a "model" of Jesus Christ?

b. How does Melchizedek's lack of "genealogy" prefigure Jesus' eternal nature?

c. Abraham is considered the Old Testament's greatest historical figure because the nation of Israel had its origin in him. But how is Melchizedek shown to be greater than Abraham?

d. One of Abraham's descendants was Levi. The descendants of Levi became Israel's priests. The people of Israel were to tithe to the priests. But, in a way, the Levites tithed to Melchizedek through their forefather Abraham's act of tithing! What does this suggest about the superiority of Melchizedek over Abraham?

e. Look at Genesis 14:18–20 once again. What does Melchizedek give Abraham? How does this foreshadow God's gift of grace in the Lord's Supper?

2. Read Hebrews 7:11–17. Hebrews refers to two different priesthoods. One priesthood originated with Aaron and was perpetually held by the Levites. Jesus, our great High Priest, was a descendant of Judah rather than Levi. In the same way, Melchizedek was not a descendant of Levi. So both Melchizedek and Jesus are depicted as members of a different kind of priesthood. Now read Hebrews 7:22–27 and explain what differences exist between these two priesthoods.

3. After reading this chapter, explain how the Old Testament sacrifices were merely "models" of Jesus' great sacrifice?

James 2: Deeds That Spring from Faith

1. Why do you think it is so tempting to treat the wealthy with more deference than the poor? How did this temptation reveal itself in the early church?

2. According to James 2:14–19, what is wrong with claiming that salvation is attained simply by knowing Jesus lived, died, and rose again? How does this help us define the essence of "faith"?

3. James points out that both Abraham's and Rahab's faiths were not simply intellectual assents to the ministry of Jesus Christ. How did their faith reveal itself in deeds?

Jude: Protect the Faith!

1. What specific problem concerns Jude according to verses 16–19. Can we learn anything else about false teachers? (See verses 4, 8.)

2. What does Jude say happened to some of the angels God created (verse 6)? How is this confirmed by 2 Peter 2:4; Revelation 12:7–9; and Isaiah 14:12–15?

> For if God did not spare angels when they sinned, but sent them to hell, putting them into gloomy dungeons to be held for judgment.
> 2 Peter 2:4

And there was war in heaven. Michael and his angels fought against the dragon, and the dragon and his angels fought back. But he was not strong enough, and they lost their place in heaven. The great dragon was hurled down—that ancient serpent called the devil, or Satan, who leads the whole world astray. He was hurled to the earth, and his angels with him. Revelation 12:7–9

> How you have fallen from heaven,
>   O morning star, son of the dawn!
> You have been cast down to the earth,
>   you who once laid low the nations!
> You said in your heart,
>   "I will ascend to heaven;
> I will raise my throne
>   above the stars of God;
> I will sit enthroned on the mount of assembly,
>   on the utmost heights of the sacred mountain.
> I will ascend above the tops of the clouds;
>   I will make myself like the Most High."
> But you are brought down to the grave,
>   to the depths of the pit. Isaiah 14:12–15

3. Read Jude 12–13. How would you describe the metaphors used here? Now look at James 3:3–12. How would you compare the use of James' metaphors with Jude's? Now look at Jesus' parable in Matthew 13:1–8. Do all these images have a common theme? What does this suggest about the relationship of Jesus with James and Jude (see Mark 6:1–3)?

That same day Jesus went out of the house and sat by the lake. Such large crowds gathered around Him that He got into a boat and sat in it, while all the people stood on the shore. Then He told them many things in parables, saying: "A farmer went out to sow his seed. As he was scattering the seed, some fell along the path, and the birds came and ate it up. Some fell on rocky places, where it did not have much soil. It sprang up quickly, because the soil was shallow. But when the sun came up, the plants were scorched, and they withered because they had no root. Other seed fell among thorns, which grew up and choked the plants. Still other seed fell on good soil, where it produced a crop—a hundred, sixty or thirty times what was sown." Matthew 13:1–8

110

Jesus left there and went to His hometown, accompanied by His disciples. When the Sabbath came, He began to teach in the synagogue, and many who heard Him were amazed.

"Where did this man get these things?" they asked. "What's this wisdom that has been given Him, that He even does miracles! Isn't this the carpenter? Isn't this Mary's son and the brother of James, Joseph, Judas and Simon? Aren't His sisters here with us?" And they took offense at Him. Mark 6:1–3

Applying the Message

1. If the Old Testament sacrifices merely foreshadowed the coming of Jesus Christ, do you think it's still necessary to offer God sacrifices for our sins? When we participate in the Lord's Supper, should we view it as a sacrifice to the Lord or a chance to receive His grace? As you answer this question, keep in mind Hebrews 7:27; 10:11–14; and Matthew 26:27–28.

Then He took the cup, gave thanks and offered it to them, saying, "Drink from it, all of you. This is My blood of the covenant, which is poured out for many for the forgiveness of sins. Matthew 26:27–28

2. Hebrews says our great high priest, Jesus, can sympathize with whatever problems we may face. Read Hebrews 4:14–16 and explain why this realization can be so comforting.

3. No one knows with certainty who wrote Hebrews. Many have claimed it was Paul. But read Hebrews 2:3 and explain why this verse seems to exclude Paul. Then look at Acts 18:24–28 and discuss why Apollos might be a good candidate for the authorship of Hebrews.

> Meanwhile a Jew named Apollos, a native of Alexandria, came to Ephesus. He was a learned man, with a thorough knowledge of the Scriptures. He had been instructed in the way of the Lord, and he spoke with great fervor and taught about Jesus accurately, though he knew only the baptism of John. He began to speak boldly in the synagogue. When Priscilla and Aquila heard him, they invited him to their home and explained to him the way of God more adequately.

> When Apollos wanted to go to Achaia, the brothers encouraged him and wrote to the disciples there to welcome him. On arriving, he was a great help to those who by grace had believed. For he vigorously refuted the Jews in public debate, proving from the Scriptures that Jesus was the Christ. Acts 18:24–28

4. If you took James 2:24 out of context, what would it suggest about "salvation by God's grace through faith in Jesus Christ"? Why is it so important to base doctrine on the New Testament as a whole rather than on selected verses?

5. In what way could the church turn the grace of God into a "license for immorality" (as described in Jude 4)? How does Paul refute that temptation in Romans 6:1–7?

> What shall we say, then? Shall we go on sinning so that grace may increase? By no means! We died to sin; how can we live in it any longer? Or don't you know that all of us who were baptized into Christ Jesus were baptized into His death? We were therefore buried with Him through baptism into death in order that, just as Christ was raised from the dead through the glory of the Father, we too may live a new life.

If we have been united with Him like this in His death, we will certainly also be united with Him in His resurrection. For we know that our old self was crucified with Him so that the body of sin might be done away with, that we should no longer be slaves to sin—because anyone who has died has been freed from sin. Romans 6:1–7

Taking the Message Home

Review

Read over Hebrews 7 once again. Compare Hebrews 7 with Hebrews 10 and consider their common themes. Then read James 2 and Jude. Examine what it means to uphold all brothers and sisters in Christ as equal, without showing anyone favoritism. Focus on the role of Christian living as the natural consequence of genuine faith.

Looking Ahead

Look at 1 Peter 4; 2 Peter 2; and 1 John 3:11–24. Write down what you believe composes the main theme of each of these references.

Working Ahead

1. Why do you think unbelievers are so hostile to Christians at times? How does the presence of a witnessing Christian affect his or her environment? If you are willing, be prepared to share a time when your Christian witness was ridiculed.

2. Compare 1 John 5:13 with John 20:30–31. Then compare John 1:1–14 with 1 John 1:1–3. How do these verses intimate the presence of a common author?

3. After reading 3 John, identify the "bad guy" and describe what he has done. Then identify the "good guy."

Old Testament Sacrifices

NAME	OT REFERENCES	ELEMENTS	PURPOSE
BURNT OFFERING	Lev 1; 6:8-13; 8:18-21; 16:24	Bull, ram or male bird (dove or young pigeon for poor); wholly consumed; no defect	Voluntary act of worship; atonement for unintentional sin in general; expression of devotion, commitment and complete surrender to God
GRAIN OFFERING	Lev 2; 6:14-23	Grain, fine flour, olive oil, incense, baked bread (cakes or wafers), salt; no yeast or honey; accompanied burnt offering and fellowship offering (along with drink offering)	Voluntary act of worship; recognition of God's goodness and provisions; devotion to God
FELLOWSHIP OFFERING	Lev 3; 7:11-34	Any animal without defect from herd or flock; variety of breads	Voluntary act of worship; thanksgiving and fellowship (it included a communal meal)
SIN OFFERING	Lev 4:1-5:13; 6:24-30; 8:14-17; 16:3-22	1. Young bull: for high priest and congregation 2. Male goat: for leader 3. Female goat or lamb: for common person 4. Dove or pigeon: for the poor 5. Tenth of an ephah of fine flour: for the very poor	Mandatory atonement for specific unintentional sin; confession of sin; forgiveness of sin; cleansing from defilement
GUILT OFFERING	Lev 5:14-6:7; 7:1-6	Ram or lamb	Mandatory atonement for unintentional sin requiring restitution; cleansing from defilement; make restitution; pay 20% fine

When more than one kind of offering was presented (as in Nu 6:16, 17), the procedure was usually as follows: (1) sin offering or guilt offering, (2) burnt offering, (3) fellowship offering and grain offering (along with a drink offering). This sequence furnishes part of the spiritual significance of the sacrificial system. First, sin had to be dealt with (sin offering or guilt offering). Second, the worshiper committed himself completely to God (burnt offering and grain offering). Third, fellowship or communion between the Lord, the priest and the worshiper (fellowship offering) was established. To state it another way, there were sacrifices of expiation (sin offerings and guilt offerings), consecration (burnt offerings and grain offerings) and communion (fellowship offerings—these included vow offerings, thank offerings and freewill offerings).

Did you know that there were three successive temples in Jerusalem, all built on approximately the same site? King Solomon built the first, which was destroyed by the Babylonians in 586 B.C. The second was built by Zerubbabel in 516 B.C. King Herod razed Zerubbabel's temple in 20 B.C. and built another which, in turn, was destroyed by the Romans in A.D. 70. No tangible vestige of any of the three remain, except a 52-yard stretch of massive limestone blocks from Herod's temple known today as "the Wailing Wall."

St. Peter and St. John at the Beautiful Gate by Gustave Doré

Then Peter said, Silver and gold have I none; but such as I have give I thee: In the name of Jesus Christ of Nazareth rise up and walk (Acts 3:6 KJV). From the *Doré Bible Illustrated*. By permission of Dover Publications, Inc.

Session 11

1–2 Peter; 1–3 John:
Letters of Suffering and Love

1 Peter 1; 2 Peter 2; 1 John 3; 2 John; 3 John

Approaching This Study

This session focuses on five short letters written by two of Jesus' most intimate disciples, Peter and John. These two disciples accompanied Jesus to the Mount of Transfiguration and were drawn apart from the other disciples by Him in the Garden of Gethsemane. They were closer to Jesus than the others.

Peter's first letter speaks about the suffering which Christians often endure for their faith. It also defines Christians as "a royal priesthood, a holy nation." Peter's second letter echoes Jude's exhortation to guard against false teaching. And as we guard the true faith, Peter asks that we remain prepared for the end of the world, which will come suddenly and without warning.

John's first letter deals primarily with love. He says that Christians reflect God's love in their relationships with other people. In his second letter, John writes to a particular "elect lady and her children" which probably refers to one of the Christian churches (the lady) and the members of the church (her children). The third letter praises a certain man named Gaius for his faith while criticizing a certain Diotrephes, who was an obstacle to the work of the church.

In many ways these two apostles write very different letters. One disciple emphasizes suffering, the other love. But both writers are influenced by their close friendship with Jesus Christ.

An Overview

Ask volunteers to read 1 Peter 1; 2 Peter 2; 1 John 3; 2 John; and 3 John. After each passage is read, share your understanding of the main themes. Pay particular attention to the differences in style between Peter's writings and John's.

117

The Roman Empire

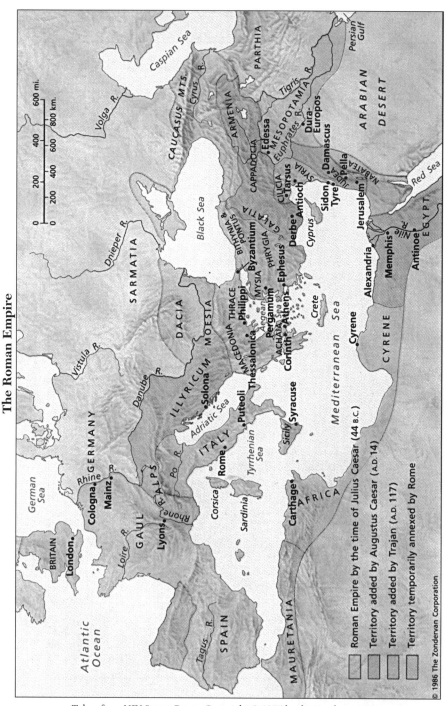

Legend:
- Roman Empire by the time of Julius Caesar (44 B.C.)
- Territory added by Augustus Caesar (A.D. 14)
- Territory added by Trajan (A.D. 117)
- Territory temporarily annexed by Rome

© 1986 The Zondervan Corporation

Taken from NIV STUDY BIBLE. Copyright © 1985 by the Zondervan Corporation.
Used by permission of Zondervan Publishing House.

The Message in Brief

As we read 1 Peter it is clear the recipients of the letter are burdened with suffering. And their suffering is being used by God to refine their faith. Peter encourages them to endure their sufferings with the help and strength of the Lord. He reminds them that they have been chosen by God to witness their faith in the midst of suffering. In his second letter, Peter warns about false teachers who have infiltrated the church. By the Spirit's power Christians should remain fortified in the will of God despite their sufferings because the Lord will return suddenly and unexpectedly.

John's letters focus on God's gift of love which is reflected in Christian living. John defines "love" as following Jesus' commands. John reflects Paul's understanding that true love is not a feeling or emotion, but a commitment. John's second and third letters are highly personal, directed toward specific problems afflicting two Christian communities.

Working with the Text

1 Peter 1: Christian Suffering

1. 1 Peter 1:1–2 states that Christians are chosen by God rather than having decided to follow Him. How is this confirmed by Paul in Ephesians 1:4–5, 11? When does Paul say Christians were chosen by God?

> For He chose us in Him before the creation of the world to be holy and blameless in His sight. In love He predestined us to be adopted as His sons through Jesus Christ, in accordance with His pleasure and will. … In Him we were also chosen, having been predestined according to the plan of Him who works out everything in conformity with the purpose of His will. Ephesians 1:4–5, 11

2. What is the reason for the difficult trials that the recipients of Peter's letters are enduring according to 1 Peter 1:6–7? Read Hebrews 12:7–11. How can tribulation actually be evidence of God's love for us? Do you find this comforting? Why or why not?

Endure hardship as discipline; God is treating you as sons. For what son is not disciplined by his father? If you are not disciplined (and everyone undergoes discipline), then you are illegitimate children and not true sons. Moreover, we have all had human fathers who disciplined us and we respected them for it. How much more should we submit to the Father of our spirits and live! Our fathers disciplined us for a little while as they thought best; but God disciplines us for our good, that we may share in His holiness. No discipline seems pleasant at the time, but painful. Later on, however, it produces a harvest of righteousness and peace for those who have been trained by it. Hebrews 12:7–11

3. According to 1 Peter 1:10–12 what was the purpose of Old Testament prophecy? Did these prophets clearly understand when the Messiah would come, sacrifice Himself for sin, and be exalted?

4. How should those who are "disciplined" in the faith through trial and tribulation respond according to 1 Peter 1:13–15?

2 Peter 2: A Warning about False Teachers

1. After reading 2 Peter 2:1–5, 10–12 explain in your own words some of the characteristics displayed by the false teachers. Are their heresies bold and up front? Are they moral? Why are they teaching things which are false? What is their attitude toward angels?

2. The full extent of the false teachers' immorality is expressed in 2 Peter 2:13–16. Describe their behavior. Are they interested in God's Law anymore? Look up Numbers 22 and scan this unique story. What was Balaam's compensation for attempting to curse the Israelites (v. 7)? What does this suggest about the motives of those false teachers in 2 Peter 2?

3. Read 2 Peter 2: 17–22. Are those who advocate sexual liberation and immorality really free? What does Peter suggest about those who follow Jesus, then fall away. Can they ever return to Him? How easy is it?

4. Turn to 2 Peter 1:16–18. What event is Peter describing? How adamant is he about the reality of this event? Why does he want us to believe him?

5. 2 Peter 3:8–10 explains why the Lord has waited so long to return. What is the reason? How is this reason consistent with a God of love? Describe in your own words what will happen when time runs out and the Lord returns.

1 John 3: a Letter about Love

1. After reading 1 John 3:4–6, how would you describe John's writing style?

2. How can we determine who is *not* a child of God according to 1 John 3:10? Since all of us fall short in doing right and loving our neighbors, to what kind of behavior do you think John refers?

3. Read 1 John 3:16–18. Who first demonstrated love to us? How do we reflect that love? Are words of love sufficient? How is true love displayed according to 1 John 5:2–3?

2 John: a Short Note about Erring Evangelists

How does 2 John 5–6 echo John's first letter? Focus on 2 John 7–11. Even in John's day there were false teachers who possessed the spirit of the "antichrist." How should Christians regard false teachers?

3 John: a Short Note to Gaius

What is Diotrephes doing wrong? Who are the "good guys" in this letter?

Applying the Message

1. Can you remember a time when you grew spiritually through the trials you faced? After thinking about this for a moment, share your thoughts and memories with the others. Tell how God molded you through your time of hardship.

2. What does it mean to you that God chose you "before the foundation of the world"? Does this give you a sense of wonderment and security? Whom does God want saved according to 1 Timothy 2:4? Look up Matthew 23:37. Why are some not saved? Whose decision is it that we follow Jesus? Whose decision that we reject Jesus?

[God] wants all men to be saved and to come to a knowledge of the truth. 1 Timothy 2:4

"O Jerusalem, Jerusalem, you who kill the prophets and stone those sent to you, how often I have longed to gather your children together, as a hen gathers her chicks under her wings, but you were not willing." Matthew 23:37

3. Think again about 2 Peter 2:17–22. Our society underwent a social upheaval in the 1960s. There was an emphasis on sexual liberation under the guise of "free love." Looking back from the 1990s, has the concept of "free love" been a success? Why or why not?

4. Look up the Ten Commandments in Exodus 20:3–17. The first three commandments are often called the "First Table of the Law" because they define our relationship with God. The last seven commandments are called the "Second Table of the Law." They define

behavior towards our neighbors. Explain how each commandment calls for service either to God or our fellowman.

"You shall have no other gods before Me.

"You shall not make for yourself an idol in the form of anything in heaven above or on the earth beneath or in the waters below. You shall not bow down to them or worship them; for I, the LORD your God, am a jealous God, punishing the children for the sin of the fathers to the third and fourth generation of those who hate Me, but showing love to a thousand generations of those who love Me and keep My commandments.

"You shall not misuse the name of the LORD your God, for the LORD will not hold anyone guiltless who misuses His name.

"Remember the Sabbath day by keeping it holy. Six days you shall labor and do all your work, but the seventh day is a Sabbath to the LORD your God. On it you shall not do any work, neither you, nor your son or daughter, nor your manservant or maidservant, nor your animals, nor the alien within your gates. For in six days the LORD made the heavens and the earth, the sea, and all that is in them, but he rested on the seventh day. Therefore the LORD blessed the Sabbath day and made it holy.

"Honor your father and your mother, so that you may live long in the land the LORD your God is giving you.

"You shall not murder.

"You shall not commit adultery.

"You shall not steal.

"You shall not give false testimony against your neighbor.

"You shall not covet your neighbor's house. You shall not covet your neighbor's wife, or his manservant or maidservant, his ox or donkey, or anything that belongs to your neighbor." Exodus 20:3–17

5. Consider some television evangelists you have watched. Who is your favorite and why? If you hear an evangelist preach false doctrine, should you support him financially? Should you support him with prayer? Why?

Taking the Message Home

Review

Read again the Scripture references studied in this session. If you have the time, read the five letters in their entirety. Refresh your memory about the themes found in each. Pay particular attention to how closely 2 Peter resembles Jude.

Looking Ahead

Revelation is a complex and mysterious book. People have interpreted its message in many different ways. Before the next session, read Revelation 12. Rewrite the chapter in your own words and describe how you feel about its images. Do they puzzle and disturb you? What do you think the purpose of such seemingly bizarre imagery might be?

Working Ahead

Choose one or more of the following for further study:

1. Before the next session, collect some political cartoons from the newspaper. Give labels to those pictures which are "symbolic" (for example, a picture of "Uncle Sam" would obviously represent the United States). Bring them to the next session to share with the others.

2. Write down your understanding of the purpose of Revelation. Does it predict the future of the world? Does it give us an historical outline of things to come? Does it indicate eternal truths about good and evil? Or is it completely indecipherable?

3. Do you have a favorite number? How about a favorite color? Why are these your favorites? What do they mean to you? After thinking about this, be prepared to share you answers at the next session. Be prepared to hear some interesting choices!

4. Read Revelation 21:1–5 and consider why these verses would be encouraging words at a funeral. How does it describe our eternal lives with the Lord? What hope does it give for the future?

Did you know that early church historians claim Peter suffered martyrdom for his faith when he was an old man in Rome? He was crucified head downwards during the reign of Emperor Nero in A.D. 64. He wished to be crucified in this position, legend has it, because he felt unworthy to die in the same position as Jesus.

Session 12

Revelation: God's Grace in Pictures

Revelation 12

Approaching This Study

Revelation is the most misunderstood book in the Bible. Over the centuries readers have debated its meaning and purpose. Some people think it predicts what will happen at the end of time. Others think it only describes what was happening in the first century, when John wrote it. Still others believe it describes a long chain of historical events from John's day to the end of history. And still others view it as symbolic of basic truths about good and evil.

Some people are tempted to interpret Revelation as a specific outline of historical events to come. When people have used the vision in such a manner, they have always been wrong. Many others have been misled by their predictions. Jesus could arrive in glory today, or He could wait another 2,000 years. And as far as our own lives are concerned, we could be taken by death and be in our eternal home at any time. The urgency we sense by reading this book isn't for Christ's second coming alone. It points us to the very real possibility that we may be with our Lord at any moment.

Lutherans have always believed difficult parts of Scripture should be interpreted by other parts of Scripture which are more understandable. "Scripture interprets Scripture." This is a good rule-of-thumb for gaining a level-headed understanding of Revelation. Rather than introducing new doctrines, Revelation confirms what the rest of the Bible has already taught.

It is best to view this book as one which employs many "pictures," or symbols, to communicate its message. This is similar to political cartoonists who use pictures to express their ideas. Sometimes we can understand the pictures used in Revelation. At other times they remain a mystery. And yet we can gain a general sense of what John wanted to say when he recorded his vision.

Overall, the best way to understand this book is to view it as a description of God granting His church victory over evil. It shows that Christ's people will ultimately be victorious even though it might appear the forces of evil are stronger.

An Overview

Read Revelation 12. When you are finished, share the images this chapter provides. Do any of them sound familiar to you? Why?

The Message in Brief

Chapter 12 provides an interesting example of "pictures" communicating a scriptural message. Through the images of a woman, an infant son, and a dragon, we gain an understanding of the devil's attacks against God's church, and we are assured that God will protect His people from the enemy.

Working with the Text

1. The first picture given us in Revelation 12:1–2 is that of a woman with 12 stars on her head who is pregnant and about to give birth. Who might she represent if this were some "political cartoon"? Consider these thoughts: (1) How many sons did Jacob have (see Genesis 35:22–26)? Remember that these sons and their descendants composed the nation of Israel. (2) How does Scripture sometimes refer to God's Old Testament people according to Isaiah 54:1–3; 66:7–11; and Micah 4:10?

> While Israel was living in that region, Reuben went in and slept with his father's concubine Bilhah, and Israel heard of it.
>
> Jacob had twelve sons:
>
> The sons of Leah: Reuben the firstborn of Jacob, Simeon, Levi, Judah, Issachar and Zebulun.
>
> The sons of Rachel: Joseph and Benjamin.
>
> The sons of Rachel's maidservant Bilhah: Dan and Naphtali.

The sons of Leah's maidservant Zilpah: Gad and Asher.

These were the sons of Jacob, who were born to him in Paddan Aram. Genesis 35:22–26

"Sing, O barren woman,
    you who never bore a child;
burst into song, shout for joy,
    you who were never in labor;
because more are the children of the desolate woman
    than of her who has a husband" says the LORD.
"Enlarge the place of your tent,
    stretch your tent curtains wide,
    do not hold back;
lengthen your cords,
    strengthen your stakes.
For you will spread out to the right and to the left;
    your descendants will dispossess nations
and settle in their desolate cities." Isaiah 54:1–3

"Before she goes into labor,
    she gives birth;
before the pains come upon her,
    she delivers a son.
Who has ever heard of such a thing?
    Who has ever seen such things?
Can a country be born in a day
    or a nation be brought forth in a moment?
Yet no sooner is Zion in labor
    than she gives birth to her children.
Do I bring to the moment of birth
    and not give delivery?" says the LORD.
"Do I close up the womb
    when I bring to delivery?" says your God.
"Rejoice with Jerusalem and be glad for her,
    all you who love her;
rejoice greatly with her,
    all you who mourn over her.
For you will nurse and be satisfied
    at her comforting breasts;
you will drink deeply and delight
    in her overflowing abundance." Isaiah 66:7–11

Writhe in agony, O Daughter of Zion, like a woman in labor, for now you must leave the city to camp in the open field. You will go to Babylon; there you will be rescued. There the LORD will redeem you out of the hand of your enemies. Micah 4:10

2. The next picture in Revelation 12:3–4 is a red dragon with 7 heads and 10 horns and 7 crowns on his heads. Who is represented by this image? (If you skip to verse 9, this should be easy.) What are its intentions according to verse 4?

3. Who immediately comes to mind when you think of "a son, a male child, who will rule all the nations with an iron scepter"? How is this supported by the messianic prophecy of Psalm 2:7–9? When the child is "snatched up to God and His throne," what event is being described (see Luke 24:50–53)? What happens to the woman? How is she protected? How does this suggest God's church is protected?

I will proclaim the decree of the LORD: He said to me, "You are my Son; today I have become your Father. Ask of Me, and I will make the nations your inheritance, the ends of the earth your possession.

You will rule them with an iron scepter; you will dash them to pieces like pottery." Psalm 2:7–9

When He had led them out to the vicinity of Bethany, He lifted up His hands and blessed them. While He was blessing them, He left them and was taken up into heaven. Then they worshiped Him and returned to Jerusalem with great joy. And they stayed continually at the temple, praising God. Luke 24:50–53

4. Describe the "heavenly battle" and what happens to the devil. How is this supported by other portions of Scripture such as Luke 10:17–18; Isaiah 14:12–15; 2 Peter 2:4; and Jude 6? Where is he hurled according to verse 9? How was he overcome according to verse 11? How does the devil feel about his defeat (verse 12)? And what are his intentions according to verse 13? How does this explain the devil's antagonism toward the church?

> The seventy-two returned with joy and said, "Lord, even the demons submit to us in Your name." He replied, "I saw Satan fall like lightning from heaven." Luke 10:17–18

> How you have fallen from heaven,
>   O morning star, son of the dawn!
> You have been cast down to the earth,
>   you who once laid low the nations!
> You said in your heart,
>   "I will ascend to heaven;
> I will raise my throne
>   above the stars of God;
> I will sit enthroned on the mount of assembly,
>   on the utmost heights of the sacred mountain.
> I will ascend above the tops of the clouds;
>   I will make myself like the Most High."
> But you are brought down to the grave,
>   to the depths of the pit. Isaiah 14:12–15

> For if God did not spare angels when they sinned, but sent them to hell, putting them into gloomy dungeons to be held for judgment. 2 Peter 2:4

> And the angels who did not keep their positions of authority but abandoned their own home—these He has kept in darkness, bound with everlasting chains for judgment on the great Day. Jude 6

5. Describe how the woman is protected by God in verse 14. Now look at Exodus 19:3–4; Psalm 91:4; and Matthew 23:37. How do these

other images support the picture of God's protection and deliverance of the woman?

> Then Moses went up to God, and the LORD called to him from the mountain and said, "This is what you are to say to the house of Jacob and what you are to tell the people of Israel: 'You yourselves have seen what I did to Egypt, and how I carried you on eagles' wings and brought you to Myself.'" Exodus 19:3–4

> He will cover you with His feathers, and under His wings you will find refuge; His faithfulness will be your shield and rampart. Psalm 91:4

> "O Jerusalem, Jerusalem, you who kill the prophets and stone those sent to you, how often I have longed to gather your children together, as a hen gathers her chicks under her wings, but you were not willing. Matthew 23:37

6. What force does the devil unleash to destroy the woman in verse 15? Then how does nature, God's creation, protect the woman (verse 16)?

7. Read verse 17. What is the dragon's reaction to this frustration? What will he attempt to do because of his anger? Who does John say comprises the woman's offspring? Again, what does this suggest about the reason for the devil's attacks against individual Christians?

8. Now, combine all the answers to the above questions and explain in your own words the meaning of chapter 12.

Applying the Message

1. Since Revelation's theme is about the victory of God's church through Jesus Christ, it makes sense that the entire book should be addressed to seven churches. Read Revelation 2–3 and list the seven churches and their problems. Can you think of any similarities between these churches and your own? Do you think most of our churches today are like these seven churches in one way or another?

2. Three times in Revelation Jesus says, "I come quickly" (Revelation 3:11, 22:7, 20). What does that mean to you?

3. Read Revelation 21:1–10. What makes heaven so wonderful? What other ideas do you gain about heaven from the following verses: 5:11–14; 7:9–12; 21:22–27?

4. Read Revelation 7:1–4 and 14:1–5. If you were to interpret Revelation without the rest of Scripture, how many people would you believe are destined to salvation? From what race must they be? How would this be a direct contradiction with Paul's words in Romans 10:12–13? What comfort does this give you?

> For there is no difference between Jew and Gentile—the same Lord is Lord of all and richly blesses all who call on Him, for, "Everyone who calls on the name of the Lord will be saved." Romans 10:12–13

5. Having learned how symbolic Revelation is, why is it dangerous to read Revelation 20:1–3 and claim that Jesus will keep the devil chained for exactly 1,000 years? What happens after "the thousand years" according to verse 3? How do you think this coincides with Jesus' warning in Matthew 24:21–22?

> "For then there will be great distress, unequaled from the beginning of the world until now—and never to be equaled again. If those days had not been cut short, no one would survive, but for the sake of the elect those days will be shortened." Matthew 24:21–22

6. The great strength of the angels is recorded in Revelation 12:7–10. After reading Psalm 91:11–12; Psalm 103:20; and 2 Thessalonians 1:7; why it is so important for Christians to know about God's angels?

> For He will command His angels concerning you
> >   to guard you in all your ways;
> they will lift you up in their hands,
> >   so that you will not strike your foot against a stone.
> Psalm 91:11–12

> Praise the LORD, you His angels, you mighty ones who do His bidding, who obey His word. Psalm 103:20

> … and give relief to you who are troubled, and to us as well. This will happen when the Lord Jesus is revealed from heaven in blazing fire with His powerful angels. 2 Thessalonians 1:7

7. Read Revelation 22:17. Why do you think Scripture has so many words of invitation?

8. We have come to the last session of this Study Guide. But this doesn't mean we've finished studying the Bible. This has only been an introduction to the New Testament books. There were many questions left unanswered and many verses left unstudied. How will you continue to study God's Word? Will you study one particular book? Will you investigate certain topics?

Explain your plan.

Taking the Message Home

Review

Spend some time and write down which books of the New Testament you enjoyed most. Why? Explain which biblical thoughts were most interesting to you.

Looking Ahead

Ask some of your brothers and sisters in Christ to join you in the further study of God's Word. Be sure to choose a time and place that is convenient for all. Then choose a particular book or topic which appeals to you. The gospel of John is a good beginning. Or you might like to study Jesus' healing ministry. Pray that the Lord motivates each one in the group to remain in the Word.

Working Ahead

1. Find information about the New Testament writers. Look up John, Peter, James, Matthew, Luke, Mark, Paul, and/or Jude in a Bible dictionary and discover more about their backgrounds.

2. Contemplate the resurrected and exalted Lord's appearance and words in Revelation 1:12–18. Consider how this picture compares with your image of Jesus from the four gospels. Think about the effect Christ's exaltation had on His authority and power.

3. Offer a prayer of thanks to the Lord for giving us His inspired Word. Consider what little we would know about God's grace without it.

Then write down how your perspective of the Lord has changed during the course of these sessions.

Did you know that there are 1,189 chapters in the Bible: 929 in the Old Testament and 260 in the New Testament? The longest chapter is Psalm 119. The shortest chapter is Psalm 117. The longest verse is Esther 8:9. The shortest verse is John 11:35.

adultery. In the Old Testament adultery refers to sexual intercourse between a man and another man's wife. Jesus interprets the Sixth Commandment as forbidding all kinds of sexual indecency in both deed and thought.

amen. The word *amen* is spoken when one wants to express "so be it." It indicates confirmation or agreement.

angels. Literally "messengers." Unseen, spiritual, holy, heavenly beings who continually do God's bidding. Angels protect and serve those who fear God. They differ in rank and dignity.

anoint. To apply oil to a person or thing. Sometimes it was simply a part of grooming. After washing or bathing, people anointed themselves. Hosts anointed their guests as an act of courtesy or respect. Anointing was also done at a person's induction to the office of priest or king. Christ was anointed with the Holy Spirit.

Antichrist. One who is both an enemy of Christ and a usurper of His rights and names.

apocalyptic literature. These include the books of Daniel and Revelation, which reveal events of the Last Times, judgment, and the hereafter. Apocalyptic literature uses numbers and symbols to express certain ideas.

Baptism. Christian Baptism must include the application of water in the name of the triune God, Father, Son, and Holy Spirit. The way the water is applied to the individual, however, can vary. The New Testament makes no distinction between adult and infant baptism. Christian baptism works the forgiveness of sins; it delivers one from spiritual death and the devil; it gives eternal salvation to all who believe in Christ; it offers the Holy Spirit. Baptism also makes one a member of the body of Christ, the church.

Christ. Greek for the Hebrew *messiah*, which means "anointed one." Jesus is the promised Messiah.

church. The collected gathering of God's people. The New Testament speaks of the church both as the Christians gathered in a specific place and as all Christians everywhere of all time. It is also described as the fellowship of God's people, the bride of Christ, the body of Christ, and a building of which Jesus Christ is the chief cornerstone.

circumcision. Removal of the foreskin of the penis. God instituted the rite of circumcision upon Abraham and his descendants. It showed that He would be their God, and they were to belong to Him. The Hebrew people looked

136

down on those who were not circumcised. Controversy erupted in the early Christian church between Jewish Christians who demanded that Gentiles be circumcised in order to be Christian and the Gentiles who refused. St. Paul spoke God's Word to this controversy when he declared that circumcision was not required of Gentiles who became Christians.

congregation. An assembly of people.

conversion. An act of God's grace by which a sinful person is turned around and brought into God's kingdom. Conversion is accomplished by the Holy Spirit, who brings the person to faith in Christ through the Word.

covenant. An agreement between two or more tribes, nations, or individuals to do or refrain from doing something.

deacon. Someone who serves. In the early church deacons were chosen to relieve the apostles of caring for the physical needs of widows and other poor people.

demons. Evil spirits who are against God and His work. They are angels who rebelled against God and now follow Satan.

doctrine. Something that is taught; instruction or teaching.

Easter. Teutonic goddess of light and spring. By the eighth century the name was applied to Christ's resurrection.

elder. In the New Testament *elder* and *bishop* are used to mean the same thing: overseer. The elder or presbyter was a man the apostles appointed in each Christian congregation to be its spiritual leader.

elect. The elect are those who have faith in Christ as the promised Messiah and Savior.

election. The New Testament spells out the doctrine of election. No one deserves to be saved. God, however, desires from eternity that all people be saved. By God's grace through faith alone in Jesus people are saved. Those who have received God's gift of faith respond in thankfulness to God for His love and grace in choosing them.

epistle. A formal letter that includes Christian doctrine and instruction.

eternal life. Eternal life begins when the Holy Spirit by grace brings a person to faith in Jesus Christ. Although the Christian already has eternal life, he or she will not experience it fully until the resurrection of the body and the life of the world to come.

faith. That belief and trust in the promise of God in Christ Jesus, worked by the Holy Spirit, through which a person is declared just, brought into a right relationship with God, saved. The Holy Spirit works faith in Christ in the individual through the Gospel and the Word and the Sacraments.

fellowship. The basic idea of fellowship is that of sharing something in common. Christian fellowship shares the common bond of the Gospel, faith in

Christ, and various spiritual gifts. Through the work of the Holy Spirit believers have a oneness in Christ.

forgiveness. God's act whereby He ends the separation caused by peoples' sins and puts them back into a proper relationship with Himself. Forgiveness is a gift of God, given out of grace for Christ's sake. As a result of Christ's forgiveness, we are to forgive our neighbor. Recognizing and being sorry for our sins precedes forgiveness.

gentiles. Non-Hebrew nations of the world. People outside the Jewish faith.

glory. That which shows the greatness of someone or something. The glory of God is shown in and by His great miracles, His eternal perfection, His creation, and all His works. Most important, it is shown by His Son, our Lord Jesus Christ.

Gnosticism. A system of belief that reached its peak in the second and third centuries. According to the Gnostics, salvation came by hating the world and everything physical and by escaping to the spirit world. They said Jesus came not to save people from sin but to show them how to escape to the spiritual world.

Gospel (Good News). The Good News that God has forgiven all people because Jesus Christ has fulfilled the Law in their place and paid the penalty for their sin on the cross.

gospels. The first four books of the New Testament. Matthew, Mark, Luke, and John each wrote one of the books. They are called gospels because they tell the good news of how salvation was won for all people by Jesus Christ.

grace. God's undeserved love and favor in Jesus Christ by which He is moved to forgive people's sins and grant them salvation. The word *grace* is sometimes used as a gift, quality, or virtue. Saving grace, however, is none of these things. It is a quality within God. It is also referred to as God's steadfast love or faithfulness.

heaven. The invisible world or universe from which God rules; the home of angels. Christ rules from heaven and receives believers there. *See also* paradise.

heir. The individual to whom another person's wealth or possessions, the person's inheritance, is given after the person dies.

hell. Either the place of eternal punishment or the punishment itself.

heresy. Stubborn error in an article of faith in opposition to Scripture.

holy. That which is set apart to be used for or by God. Holiness is the state of being without sin. The holiness of God is imparted to people through His act of choosing them in grace and through His other mighty acts. It culminates in the saving work of Jesus Christ.

hymn. A song telling about God and praising Him.

inspiration. The special way the Holy Spirit worked in certain people to cause them to act out, speak, or write God's Word. When the Holy Spirit did this, the person who was inspired was certainly under the direction of God's power (God-breathed), but he or she was not a robot.

Israel. (1) The name given to Jacob after he wrestled with an intruder (Genesis 32:28): (2) The name of the nation composed of the descendants of Jacob and his 12 sons. Jacob and his sons founded the 12 tribes of Israel. (3) The name given to the 10 northern tribes of Israel after Solomon's death, when they revolted under Rehoboam and the kingdom split in two. The Northern Kingdom was called Israel to distinguish it from the Southern Kingdom, which was called Judah. (4) This name is also used to describe all who follow in the faith of Abraham, Isaac, and Jacob and therefore are true Israelites, no matter what their physical descent.

Jesus. Greek for the Hebrew name *Joshua,* which means "savior."

Jew. Originally someone who belonged to the tribe or Kingdom of Judah as opposed to those in the Northern Kingdom. *Hebrew* denotes those who descended from Abraham; *Israel* denotes those who descended from Jacob; and *Jew* denotes those who descended from the tribe or Kingdom of Judah.

Jordan River. The most important river in Palestine. It is the river in which Jesus was baptized by John. The river is 3 to 10 feet deep and about 100 feet wide.

Judah. (1) The fourth son of Jacob and Leah. Jacob bestowed the blessing of the birthright on Judah. Jesus was one of Judah's descendants. (2) The tribe that descended from Judah. It occupied the greater part of southern Palestine. (3) The kingdom of Judah which began when the 10 northern tribes withdrew from Rehoboam around 912 B.C. and lasted until 587 B.C., when Jerusalem fell. It existed in the southern part of Palestine.

justification. The gracious act of God by which He pronounces all people to be not guilty of their sin through faith in Jesus. The basis for His acquittal is that Jesus Christ fulfilled the Law in humanity's place and paid the penalty for all people's sin as He suffered and died on the cross.

kingdom of God. A spiritual kingdom that includes all nations. The New Testament pictures God's kingdom as the Holy Spirit in the hearts of His people. The kingdom of God is, at times, spoken of as a future blessing, as in the kingdom Jesus will bring on the Last Day, and, at times, as a present reality. The church proclaims the kingdom of God by preaching the Gospel.

Lord. (1) LORD (often printed in capital and small capital letters in the Bible) is God's personal name. It comes from the Hebrew word *Yahweh.* (2.) Lord (capital *L* and the remaining letters lowercase) comes from the Hebrew word *adon.* It means "master" and denotes ownership. (3) *Adonai* is the word the Israelites said whenever they saw the consonants of Yahweh

(YHWH). (4) The Greek word *kyrios* is also translated as Lord. It is the word used for a human master or for God as the ruler. It is also the word used for Christ, who by His death and resurrection is Lord.

Lord's Supper. Christ instituted this supper on the night of His betrayal to replace the Passover feast. It is a memorial for His death for the sins of the world. In this meal Christ gives His body and blood together in, with, and under the bread and wine. Christians who trust in the blessings Christ promises to give in this meal and partake of it in faith receive the forgiveness of sins, life, and salvation, and a strengthening of their faith. Also called "Breaking of Bread," "Holy Communion," "Eucharist," and "the Lord's Table."

love. Various types of love are referred to in the Bible. The Greek word *agape* represents God's love for sinful people. This is the kind of love Christians are to have.

mercy. God's undeserved favor and love within the covenant relationship.

Messiah. Hebrew for "the anointed one." *See* Christ.

minister. A person who has been called—by God, through the church—to active service to God. All Christians have vocations—callings by God in life; and all baptized Christians have received various gifts of the Holy Spirit. All Christians are members of the priesthood of all believers (1 Peter 2:9). However, ministers have a distinct calling from God, even as Jesus chose 12 of His disciples to serve as apostles.

miracle. An event that causes wonder; something that takes place outside of the laws of nature. The New Testament depicts miracles as acts of power, signs, and wonders. Their significance could be understood only by those who had faith in Jesus Christ.

ordination. A rite (act) of the church by which the church through a congregation publicly confers the pastoral office on a qualified man. Ordination has its historical roots in the New Testament and in the early church. In the New Testament, deacons, missionaries, and elders were called to their offices, just as today a congregation calls a man to be its pastor.

parable. A method of speech that compares two objects for the purpose of teaching a moral or religious truth. It is an earthly story with a heavenly or spiritual meaning. Although the events and characters in the parable are true to nature, not every detail of the story has a spiritual meaning. Rather there is only one main point of comparison. Jesus often spoke in parables to teach the people about Himself and the kingdom of heaven.

paradise. Used in the New Testament to describe heaven, the home of those who die in Christ.

peace. Often used to describe that state of spiritual tranquility and harmony that God gives when He brings one into a right relationship with Himself.

Pentecost. The Jewish Feast of Weeks, which was celebrated 50 days after the Feast of Passover. It is also known as the Feast of Harvest and the Day of Firstfruits. On this day the Holy Spirit was outpoured on the disciples, and many people came to faith in Christ.

prayer. Speaking with God. Prayers can be formal or spoken freely from one's own thoughts and concerns. They can be said together by a large group of believers or alone by an individual. They can be said at set times and places or all times and places.

priest. One who represents the people before God. Through Moses, God appointed Aaron and his descendants as priests. They wore special clothing in the sanctuary, taught the people, and inquired of God's will. The chief priest, or high priest, was in charge of all the other priests. He offered the sin offering, made sacrifice on the Day of Atonement, and discovered the will of God through Urim and Thummim. In the New Testament, Jesus Christ is the only high priest. Since He sacrificed Himself for the sins of the people and this sacrifice need never be repeated, there is no longer a need for the Levitical priesthood. The New Testament also teaches the priesthood of all believers. Christians share in Christ's priestly activity by bringing the Gospel to people.

Redeemer, redemption. The buying back of humanity from sin and death by Christ, who paid the price with His perfect obedience and His sacrificial death on the cross.

repentance. A total change of heart and life that God works in an individual who does not believe or trust in Him by turning him or her around to one who does believe and trust in Him. Repentance includes both sorrow for one's sins and faith in Christ through whom forgiveness is granted.

resurrection. A return to life after one has died.

righteous. That which is right in accordance with the Law. The term is particularly used to describe people who are in a right relationship with God through faith.

sacrament. A word the church uses to describe a sacred act instituted by God where there are visible means connected to His Word. In a sacrament God offers, gives, and seals to the individual the forgiveness of sins earned by Christ.

sacrifice. An act of worship where a person presents an offering to God. Sacrifices were practiced from ancient times to atone for sins and to express thankfulness to God. Sacrifices were offered for various purposes. Among the main ones mentioned in the Old Testament are the sin offering, the trespass offering, the burnt offering, the peace offering, the meal and drink offerings, and the heifer offering. Offerings were sacrificed on the altar morning and evening, at each Sabbath and new moon, and at the three leading festivals. All sacrifices point to and are fulfilled in Christ, the Lamb of God, sacrificed for the sins of the world.

salvation. Deliverance from any type of evil, both physical and spiritual. Spiritual salvation includes rescue from sin. It is a gift of God's grace through faith in Christ.

Satan. The chief fallen angel and enemy of God, humanity, and all that is good. Sometimes called Abaddon, Apollyon, or Beelzebul.

Son of Man. Jesus used this title to emphasize the power and dominion He receives from the Ancient of Days. (See Daniel 7 and Matthew 16:27.)

Son of God. The title is applied to Jesus in a unique sense. It says that Jesus as the Son is equal to God the Father.

suffering servant. Jesus is the fulfillment of the suffering servant spoken about in the Old Testament (Isaiah 42:1–4, 52:13–53:12).

sin. Sin is both doing what God forbids and failing to do what He commands. Because of sin everyone deserves temporal and eternal death. Only through faith in Christ, who kept God's Law perfectly and suffered the punishment for the sins of the world, does one escape the results of sin.

soul, spirit. The soul is not separate from the body; rather it is that which gives life: it animates the flesh. It is the inner person as distinguished from the flesh. The soul departs at death. It is the seat of the appetites, emotions, and passions. It can be lost and saved.

tabernacle. The movable sanctuary in the form of a tent.

temple. The fixed sanctuary of the Lord.

testament. *See* covenant.

tithe. A tenth part of one's income. According to the Law, a tenth of all produce of land and herds was sacred to the Lord.

transfiguration. The name given to the time when Jesus was visibly glorified in the presence of His three disciples.

trinity. The church's term for the coexistence of Father, Son, and Holy Spirit in the unity of the Godhead; three distinct Persons in one divine Being, or Essence. The term *Trinity* does not occur in the Bible, but many passages support the doctrine of the Trinity.

unleavened. Bread without yeast. The Israelites ate unleavened bread at Passover as a reminder of the Exodus.

will. Inclination or choice. God's will is that which He determines. It is revealed in His acts, His Law, and especially in Christ. Humanity's fallen or natural will cannot will good. God's grace alone is able to incline a person's will to good.

Word. God's Word comes to people in various forms, for example, through speaking, writing, visions, and symbols. Jesus Christ is the supreme revelation of God. He is the living Word.

works. Whether a person's works are good or bad depends on that person's relationship to God. Only a person who believes in Jesus Christ as Savior can do good works in God's eyes, since good works are a fruit of faith.

world. Used not only to describe the universe or the human race, but often to denote the wicked and unregenerate, those who are opposed to God.

worship. To bow down, kiss the hand, to revere, work, serve. The respect and reverence given to God. New Testament worship is centered in and around the Word of God. It involved reading Scripture and psalms, singing hymns and spiritual songs, teaching, praying, and celebrating the Lord's Supper.